Gentrification Down the Shore

Gentrification Down the Shore

MOLLY VOLLMAN MAKRIS
AND MARY GATTA

Rutgers University Press
New Brunswick, Camden, and Newark, New Jersey, and London

Library of Congress Cataloging-in-Publication Data

Names: Makris, Molly Vollman, 1981– author. | Gatta, Mary Lizabeth, 1972– author.
Title: Gentrification down the shore / by Molly Vollman Makris and Mary Gatta.
Description: New Brunswick : Rutgers University Press, 2020.
| Includes bibliographical references and index.
Identifiers: LCCN 2020005638 | ISBN 9781978813618 (paperback)
| ISBN 9781978813625 (cloth) | ISBN 9781978813632 (epub) |
ISBN 9781978813649 (mobi) | ISBN 9781978813656 (pdf)
Subjects: LCSH: Gentrification—New Jersey—Asbury Park. | Sociology,
Urban—New Jersey—Asbury Park. | Asbury Park (N.J.)—Economic conditions.
Classification: LCC HT177.A76 M35 2020 | DDC 307.7609749/46—dc23
LC record available at https://lccn.loc.gov/2020005638

A British Cataloging-in-Publication record for this
book is available from the British Library.

♾ The paper used in this publication meets the requirements of the
American National Standard for Information Sciences—Permanence
of Paper for Printed Library Materials, ANSI Z39.48-1992.

www.rutgersuniversitypress.org

Manufactured in the United States of America

To the residents of Asbury Park, and residents and lovers of cities everywhere, who are fighting to keep these spaces interesting, diverse, and accepting

To Eileen and Rudy, I love you

and

To the memory of Dr. William Helmreich, who showed us the invaluable importance of walking cities and listening to locals
—MVM

To the memory of Paul Frankel, a scholar of the law and an aficionado of history whose intellectual curiosity is fondly remembered

and

To the memory of Dr. Henry Plotkin, a steadfast advocate for New Jersey's workers whose impact is everlasting
—MG

Contents

Gentrification Down the Shore

1

Seasonal Gentrification

As I approach the Asbury Park Convention Hall on this cool, overcast day, I pass the looming statue of James A. Bradley—the town founder of Asbury Park. This statue is more noticeable to me today than during other visits. The statue has been in the news and plastered on social media because a group of local residents is fighting to remove the statue because of the history of segregation and racism tied to Bradley.

I pass the statue and approach the convention center for the Catsbury Park Cat Convention. Here a number of hipsters are making their way in. I walk beside some tattooed, T-shirt wearing parents with stylishly funky children gripping cat stuffed animals. Inside the Cat Convention, there are booths with original cat art, trendy cat toys in the shape of taco seasoning, raw cat food, pet beverages, and cat bowties. The crowd is predominantly made up of White twenty- to thirty-somethings, often in trendy cat headbands or dresses with colorful hairstreaks . . . and there are a lot of beards. In the background is the distinct buzzing sound of the tattoo artists at work. This noise mixes in the room with conversations about bands and the sharing of tattoo styles and tips.

When I leave the convention center, my cat lollipops in hand, I realize that Bradley—looking out to the ocean, facing the beautiful boardwalk and iconic entertainment venues of Asbury Park—has his back turned on the west side of town.

—adapted from field notes, 2018

FIG. 1. Bradley statue. Photograph by Molly Vollman Makris, April 7, 2018.

In the late nineteenth and early twentieth centuries, Asbury Park, New Jersey—a small beachfront city on the Jersey Shore—was booming. Considered a dynamic new resort community, it was a place of leisure, with live entertainment, an arcade, and a sprawling boardwalk along with two hundred hotels and restaurants.[1] Even in its earliest days, Asbury Park had a reputation for being quirky and unusual, with cheap amusements, "wild attractions," and vendors selling "exotic" international items.[2] But not everyone enjoyed access to the amenities Asbury Park had to offer. While they toiled as waiters, entertainers, desk clerks, busboys, dishwashers, and housekeepers in the establishments that attracted vacationers to the city, Black workers were not welcome on the beaches or permitted to live on the beachfront East Side. As time wore on, Asbury Park came to illustrate the macro social and economic structural changes occurring in cities across the United States with its own beachfront twist. While Asbury Park was a popular vacation destination in the early twentieth century for White tourists, by the second half of the century, the city lost its glamour. As late as 2000, the city was still synonymous for many with violence, drugs, and crime.

Yet by 2019, Asbury Park's narrative had shifted once again. Named among the coolest small towns in the United States, the city's multi-million-dollar beachfront condos attract the attention of Hollywood stars. Summer days in Asbury once again mean tourists strolling the boardwalk, basking in the Jersey sun, and dining by the Atlantic Ocean. But less than a mile away from the seasonal crowds, many of Asbury's longtime residents live below the poverty line and struggle for their share of this prosperity.

This book captures the story of Asbury Park, which serves as an example of seasonal gentrification. The term *gentrification* has been employed with increasing frequency by urban dwellers, researchers, and journalists since its first use fifty-five years ago. While exact definitions of the term differ and scholars debate about whether the phenomenon should be characterized based on its "causes, outcomes, or everyday character,"[3] an inclusive definition from Gina Perez describes *gentrification* as "an economic and social process whereby private capital (real estate firms, developers) and individual homeowners and renters reinvest in fiscally neglected neighborhoods through housing rehabilitation, loft conversions, and the construction of new housing stock . . . gentrification is a gradual process . . . slowly reconfiguring the neighborhood landscape of consumption and residence by displacing poor and working-class residents unable to afford to live in 'revitalized' neighborhoods with rising rents, property taxes, and new businesses catering to an upscale clientele."[4]

In regard to the seasonal gentrification, which this book examines, Perez's definition warrants more delineation. In Asbury Park, the growing gentrifier population (largely tourists and second-home owners) flood the city during summer to take advantage of the beach, while longtime residents (many low-income people of color) struggle to survive economically year-round. While there has been much written on gentrifying cities and gentrification's impact on longtime residents, there has been scant attention to what happens when a city *seasonally* gentrifies. This book aims to expand the gentrification literature by looking closely at the particularities of this process when it occurs in a beach-community city. We know very little about what happens when the gentrifying populations are largely seasonal and thus less invested in year-round institutions and needs (such as the success of the city's workforce, educational system, and inequities). In this book, we utilize a framework of intersectionality—the overlap of identities and discrimination across race, class, gender, sexuality, and other identities—to help explain how residents and businesses impact and are impacted by seasonality and gentrification. We will explore Asbury Park's historically rooted socioeconomic and racial divides as well as its reputation as a space for LGBTQ visitors and residents. Using in-depth qualitative research, our book illustrates that while the gentrification may be seasonal, its effects are lasting.

Asbury Park Today: A Story of Differences

In 2016, when we began our research, Asbury Park (population of about 15,500) was experiencing renewed attention. The "Coolest Small Town in America" is once again known for its quirky feel and beachfront beauty.[5] On any given summer day, the city is flooded with LGBTQ owners of old Victorian homes, hipsters enjoying brunch en masse on Cookman Avenue, and well-heeled families from New York City and the surrounding area filling the

FIG. 2. Railroad tracks. Photograph by Erika Bentley Leonard, September 10, 2019.

boardwalk with their beach gear and strollers. The city is divided along a railroad track that is symbolic of the larger East Side–West Side division. The rapid gentrification of the East Side, which is closest to the ocean, is on the minds of residents across the city. Asbury Park, however, is still the poorest city in its county, and its Black and Brown residents continue to experience exclusion from popular East Side amenities. As one community activist explains, "Once you get off the train, like you can definitely see it. You can look on one side and it looks a whole lot brighter than the other side, and it's like once you even get off the train, like all signs are pointing to go to this way. Stay away from that way!"

Similar to other cities, the railroad tracks are not just a geographic boundary; they also exemplify a palpable social and emotional schism. While the East Side is rapidly gentrifying, the West Side is home to a largely socioeconomically disadvantaged Black and Brown population. As one young Black man from the West Side explains about the emotional difficulty of crossing over this line, "It's tough to make it across the railroad tracks because now

FIG. 3. Main Street, Asbury Park's chief north-south thoroughfare, and the New Jersey Transit train tracks, which run parallel to and one block west of Main Street, divide the city into the East Side and West Side. Map generated using U.S. Census Bureau American FactFinder.

you've got all this new stuff going on. Besides the apartments that they're building, it's beautiful . . . over there by Cookman [East Side], you've got a sense of hope."

While East Side residents complain about new luxury developments, privatization of the beach, and the lack of parking, those on the West Side worry most about crime and the lack of educational and employment opportunities. In a diverse community like this one, it is not surprising that there are ethnic tensions and frustrations that surface around issues of education, employment, housing, and race. As one West Side resident sums it up in a focus group:

All this shit right here? This is the picture that needs to be taken [for your research]. We are hurting, and we—our kids are hurting, getting locked up, everything. They have nothing to offer [us] . . . nothing to offer our kids, [our kids are] getting locked up, run the jail, they're selling drugs and everything, and they can't help them. The school system, all this, they down falling on us—they are blocking us so we can't go through, and now it's time to make a breakthrough because God is tired. We are tired. We are able and we are very educated, but they [employers] gotta block us and give [the jobs] to the Mexicans.

This quote captures a great deal of the tensions we will explore in this book. This is a town where you can purchase a top-shelf martini and sip it at a bar overlooking the Atlantic Ocean while just a few blocks away, residents live in poverty and report the noise of gunshots. During our research, we heard repeatedly about the lack of new development on the West Side. As one activist puts it, "Yeah, my issue is whose term is 'redevelopment of Asbury Park'? The first issue with that is when I hear [about the] redevelopment of a city, I would anticipate that the entire city, the four quadrants—that redevelopment would be happening everywhere. It is not." There is also concern that the development on the East Side will drive up rent prices and lead to displacement throughout town.

The gentrification described by residents on the ground is supported by numbers from the U.S. Census Bureau. As illustrated in figure 4, between 2010 and 2017, the Black / African American population in Asbury decreased by 11.1 percentage points while the White population increased by 7.4 percentage points. In 2010, 16 percent of Asbury Park's population had a bachelor's degree or higher, and by 2017, this number climbed to 23 percent. Those without a high school diploma decreased from 26 percent to 16 percent of the city's residents in those same years.[6] There has been an approximate 6 percentage point increase in employment in management, business, science, and arts and a 6 percentage point decrease in employment in natural resources, construction, and maintenance between 2008 and 2017.[7] Thus Asbury is becoming whiter and less Black / African American, and it now has more college-educated white-collar residents.

While there are new homeowners in Asbury Park, it is unlikely that they represent longtime working-class residents. In a city with a median household income of $39,324, between 2007 and

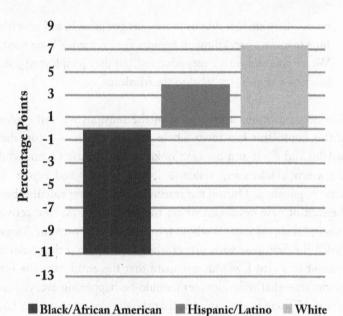

Black/African American **Hispanic/Latino** White

FIG. 4. Change in Asbury Park's racial composition, 2010–2017.
(Sources: U.S. Census Bureau, 2010 Census; and *2013–2017 American
Community Survey 5-Year Estimates*)

2017, the average home loan applicant's reported annual income
was $180,036, and by 2017, the median value of an owner-occupied
home was $335,500.[8] Rents are also increasing. The proportion of
rental units renting for $500–$999 decreased from 29.7 percent
to 19.9 percent between 2008 and 2017, while the percentage of
units renting for $1,500 or more increased from 16.9 percent to
26.3 percent.[9] Further, between 2010 and 2017, 43.1 percent of home
loan applications in the city were made for non-owner-occupied
homes.[10]

Certain populations may be more at risk of displacement or
losing their representation in the community. Between 2000 and
2017, African Americans without a high school diploma fell from
33 percent to 16 percent, while the proportion of African Americans with bachelor's degrees increased by just over 1 percentage
point, to 9.5 percent.[11] Meanwhile, the proportion of White residents with college degrees increased by 29 percentage points, to

48 percent. Children younger than nineteen fell from 32.6 percent to 25.3 percent of the city's population, while the proportion of middle-aged residents grew.[12] Yet even as vulnerable populations appear to leave the city, poverty rates remain incredibly high. In 2017, the senior poverty rate in Asbury Park was 18.1 percent and child poverty was 49.5 percent, up 4.6 percentage points since 2008.[13]

While the numbers clearly demonstrate gentrification, there are two weaknesses within the quantitative data on Asbury Park's changes. The first is that *seasonal* gentrification is more difficult to quantify than gentrification elsewhere. This is because many seasonal gentrifiers own vacation homes and long- and short-term rental units. They are counted in the geographic area of the Census where they own their primary homes, not in Asbury. Therefore, it is likely that our numbers do not include a seasonal, higher-income portion of the city's residents and underestimate shifting demographics. This illustrates an incomplete data picture, which then influences policies and regulations that require affordable housing based on demographics, since the higher-income population may be underestimated or misunderstood by local government officials and policy makers.

The second weakness within the data relates to Asbury Park's size. Since the city was home to between 16,118 (2010) and 15,511 (2018) residents during the period studied, Census Bureau demographic, employment, and income estimates have potentially large margins of error. To reduce these margins, we typically use the American Community Survey (ACS) five-year estimates; these potential margins of error are not large enough to affect the greater trends we identify or the conclusions we draw regarding gentrification. However, where we look at data on smaller subsets of the city's population or housing market, these margins can be substantial.[14]

The "Other Side of the Tracks"

In addition to the uneven redevelopment of the community and shifting demographics, while there is no signage expressly prohibiting

West Siders from accessing the East Side (as there was in the past), low-income residents of Asbury Park's West Side are still excluded from opportunities on the East Side today. As chapter 5 explains in more detail, during our research, we were told that West Side residents often do not use the beaches until the evening, when they are no longer required to pay for admittance. Other West Siders told us they never visit the beach because of the high cost of parking on the East Side and the police scrutiny they experience on that side of town. As one resident from the West Side explains, "It's too racist . . . because if you go down there, you're not dressed right. You don't look right. [Police ask,] 'What are you doing this way? Why are you over here?' You know they are stopping [people]; they're asking for ID."

Still today, many of the Black and Brown residents of Asbury Park struggle to find employment on the burgeoning East Side. As will be explored more in chapter 3, the new service sector is staffed (at least in the front of the house) largely by White, middle-class, millennial hipsters, not adults of color from the West Side. While the city opens new hotels, restaurants, stores, and bars, this development is not creating ample employment opportunities for adult West Side residents of color. If you pop into one of the many coffee shops, trendy bars, or fashionable boardwalk shops in Asbury Park, you will likely find a hip White employee staffing the visible positions (or a hip young person of color, a dynamic we will explore more in chapters 3 and 4). Additionally, while Asbury Park is now often ranked among the best beaches and vacation destinations in the country, it was also ranked in the top fifty worst places to live due to rankings based on poverty rate, crime rate, typical household income, and high cost of living.[15] The city and thus this story are complex, nuanced, and intersectional.

A New Caliber of Living

Asbury Park is experiencing a moment. In 2019, boardwalk development is moving full speed ahead while activists (like Save Asbury's Waterfront) push back against the privatization of the beachfront

FIG. 5. Asbury Ocean Club. Photograph by Erika Bentley Leonard, September 10, 2019.

and the development of private pools.[16] The most expensive development in Asbury Park, the seventeen-story Asbury Ocean Club, is described by its branding and marketing firm as "offer[ing] a new caliber of living on the Jersey Coast"[17] and by the chief executive officer of the developer iStar as "bring[ing] a whole new meaning to living both the beach life and the high life."[18] Current listings (2019) in this development are between $897,000 and $5,980,000.

As one community activist explains,

> I have heard more people speak critically about where the city is heading—and in particular, being critical of it in a negative way and using that word *gentrification* since that structural steel started to fill out on the ocean [Asbury Ocean Club]. Gentrification, I think, was probably on the minds of some people, but deep in the background. As that thing rose, story upon story upon story, it became very apparent to some that it's going to change the community, and it's . . . a signal that it's no longer going to be a place for me.

Not only are high-rise condominiums moving to the oceanfront; other changes have occurred that affect day-to-day living. For example, the city has a much-discussed ban on aggressive panhandling that is criticized as unconstitutional and unfair to the socioeconomically disadvantaged.[19] In 2018, a smoking ban for the beaches was cited by the deputy mayor as "excessive."[20]

Gentrification has not raised home values in the city's mostly Black southwest neighborhoods, and over the last decade, people of color have been poorly represented among the city's new homeowners. As figure 6 illustrates, home purchases between 2007 and 2017 have been uneven across the city, with Census tracts 8070.03/.04 on the East Side experiencing very different home purchasing than those on the southwest side (tracts 8072 and 8073). Northwest Asbury (tract 8071, an area that experienced early gentrification and gut renovations) has also seen a lot of activity.[21]

Black and Hispanic homebuyers made up just 5 percent of loan applicants in the East Side Census tracts and 10 percent in the gentrified West Side tract 8071. Even in tracts 8072 and 8073, where Black residents have historically comprised a large majority, people of color were just 35 percent and 34 percent of loan applicants, respectively.[22]

Black homeownership has fallen in all five Asbury Park Census tracts since the turn of the century, and the Census Bureau estimates that as of 2017, there were *no* Black / African American homeowners in Asbury Park's two seaside tracts. The number of Black renters has also fallen in the gentrified tracts 8070.03, 8070.04, and 8071 while remaining essentially the same in the city's southwest.[23] As illustrated in figures 7 and 8, African Americans contribute much smaller percentages of the city's population in all five Census tracts than they did two decades ago.

Policy makers are discussing demographic disparities in the city, but much work remains. Beth McManus, Asbury Park's external affordable housing consultant, explains in *triCityNews*, "Asbury Park is one of the few municipalities that are interested in going above and beyond their affordable housing obligation."[24] The city's planning board adopted a new housing element for the

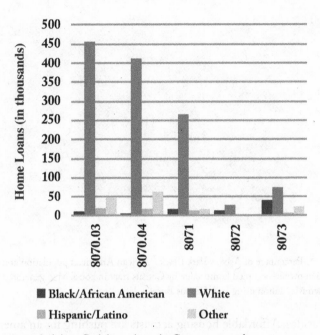

FIG. 6. Asbury Park home loans by Census tract and race, 2007–2017. (Source: U.S. Consumer Financial Protection Bureau, HMDA Loan/Application Register data for the years cited)

master plan (which will need to be approved by a state judge and then enacted by the council), and the political consensus behind this plan demonstrates the board's commitment. It will allow for increased densities in certain areas with 15 percent set-asides for low- and moderate-income housing. In the downtown business district, it will loosen nonresident parking requirements and allowable height restrictions for 10 percent low- and moderate-income housing set-asides. There will also be incentives for more affordable housing on the West Side in the Springwood Avenue and Washington Avenue redevelopment areas.[25] This is not enough. When it comes to the waterfront, however, this work is even more challenging. That area of development is part of a binding agreement with the official waterfront developer, iStar. This New York City–based real estate firm took control of waterfront redevelopment in 2009 after many stops and starts. iStar now pays into a city fund that can be used for affordable housing but does not include

FIG. 7. Percentage of Asbury Park Black / African American population and median owner-occupied home value by Census tract in 2000. Map generated by Shawn McMahon using U.S. Census Bureau data.

set-asides. Affordable housing activists are pushing for an amendment to this agreement to ensure that there is affordable housing in the area "where more than 50 percent of the City's new development will be created."[26] Asbury Park officials are also looking to purchase land to prevent iStar from building sixteen town houses on the beach.[27]

This is a moment when the city's future is uncertain, but its believers and activists hope to maintain its funky vibe, socioeconomic and racial diversity, small business community, and reputation as a safe powerful hub for the LGBTQ community. They want to see a West Side that is vibrant, safe, and supportive of longtime residents of color. At the moment, several questions remain. With the eyes and capital of developers and wealthy out-of-towners in play, can Asbury Park resist the path of its East Coast neighbors like Hoboken, New Jersey; the Meatpacking District in Manhattan; and Williamsburg, Brooklyn? We argue that with historically rooted racism and capitalist interests at play, public officials and activists will need to carve out a path that will not just reward the advantaged and hurt the most vulnerable. As one of our participants says, "So when you see people on this side

FIG. 8. Percentage of Asbury Park Black / African American population and median owner-occupied home value by Census tract in 2017. Map generated by Shawn McMahon using U.S. Census Bureau data.

of town, not just Black people but Spanish people—and I'm gonna just be quite honest, poor White people—and they watch one side of town being built, you know, and the other side of town, they just hear empty promises. . . . They have reached a point where there is no belief."

Seasonal Gentrification and Labor

Our Asbury Park story is not just about gentrification; it is about what happens when a city seasonally gentrifies. Since its original use by Ruth Glass in 1964, *gentrification* has become a term that is so frequently used, scholars have begun to question its worth. As the authors of *Gentrifier* state, "Myriad diverse urban issues have been subsumed under the gentrification umbrella."[28] Yet despite this attention, the relationship between gentrification and the local labor market is a significantly underresearched area of the gentrification literature.

There *has* been a great deal of attention paid to the impact on property taxes for local government, crime rates, revitalized streets, improvements in physical infrastructure, and the preservation of historic properties as a result of gentrification.[29] Critics of gentrification have painstakingly highlighted the social costs of neighborhood change and its effects on the political power and quality of life for longtime residents and the resultant policing of people of color. They have also noted how the displacement of low- and moderate-income households exacerbates affordable housing problems, destroys long-standing social ties, can lead to homelessness, and causes the resegregation of urban housing markets and inequality within and between schools.[30] Scholars have examined the causes of gentrification from the individual to the market to the role of the state.[31] However, what is missing from much of this literature is the connection between jobs and gentrification—specifically, how employment is affected for local residents who remain in the community during and postgentrification.

Complicating our research even more is that there is a dearth of studies on seasonal gentrification. We define *seasonal gentrification* as gentrification in which there is a transition from a low-income or working-class community to a middle-class or upper-class community increasingly composed of second-home owners and vacationers (both day-trippers and seasonal visitors). These seasonal homes and businesses catering to vacationers (such as hotels, boardwalk stores, and restaurants) are used by the in-comers more heavily during certain months of the year, which affects all areas of development (e.g., education, employment opportunities, and the types of amenities that open). Seasonal gentrifiers differ from longtime residents in their socioeconomic and racial/ethnic backgrounds.

Scholars examining a related phenomenon in mountain towns with ski tourism have identified "amenity-led migration," or migration for pleasure, and there has been some investigation into the similar idea of wilderness gentrification.[32] Manfred Perlik has demonstrated how technology enables this movement toward second-home ownership, as individuals can maintain networks in their central metropolis from a seasonal home. He states that while this kind of migration might seem to be a rural phenomenon, it stems from an urban outlook: "Dwelling in the mountains is not a tendency of rural life but an urban attitude in provenance and character."[33] Moreover, Chris Paris argues that "the growth of second home ownership is conceptualized as a form of gentrification. . . . Household investment and consumption strategies, fueled by greater mobility and hyper-consumption capacities in rich countries, are seen to be at the core of this rapidly evolving phenomenon."[34]

Asbury Park on the Jersey Shore is within the larger New York metropolitan area (and transportation network), making it an ideal location for urban dwellers with this "urban attitude" to get away or own a second home less than two hours by train or car from New York City. While it is more affordable than gentrified New York City or the Hamptons, those who can vacation or own seasonal homes in Asbury Park generally have significantly more economic capital and ability for consumption than do local residents. There is also a racial shift that is occurring with the gentrification of Asbury Park, as longtime residents who remained in the city throughout the century are largely people of color, and the newcomers are mainly White. Like other cases of gentrification, race is a component that cannot be overstated.[35] Other historically African American beach towns, such as the Sea Islands in North Carolina and Sag Harbor Hills in the Hamptons, have experienced these racial changes as property value in these locations increases.[36]

As income gaps widen, technology advances, and wealth in global cities like New York increases, there will be more seasonal gentrification—and with it, displacement of Black and Brown working-class and low-income communities in larger metropolitan areas.[37] This research contributes to the literature by offering insight into the seasonal gentrification of a beach city.

While Asbury Park has always been divided between haves and have-nots and along racial lines, what is occurring in the twenty-first century is a marked change—particularly because in recent generations, the city was not the tourist destination it is (again) now. The amount of capital coming into the community has increased exponentially, and more wealthy residents are purchasing homes. Meanwhile, service-sector hospitality jobs are not creating sustainable employment paths for longtime residents of color. This is especially evident in the context of seasonal gentrification. As the city gentrifies, the available jobs are also often seasonal, and they are in the restaurants, hotels, and boutiques, where a key aspect is the "brand" that is being sold. As we explore in chapter 3, many West Side residents, regardless of education and training, may not be able to achieve the aesthetic labor that is often required in these positions. In the older seasonal order, White tourists expected and welcomed servile labor from Black workers. But in the new order, creative-class tourists may expect something else—the "cool" mixologist bartender or the hipster coffee barista. West Side residents today do not feel like they have access to these jobs. They face significant barriers that stem from today's systemic inequities, with additional competition from educated White millennials. Yet within the context of seasonal work and inequality, aesthetic labor demands brought about by gentrification further limit the opportunities of longtime residents of color.

Those who support new economic development in urban spaces often tout the increased opportunities for employment. It is known that economic change in a community brings new retail businesses.[38] Yet gentrification is associated with industrial restructuring, and as a result, people move toward jobs, and new residents create competition for employment.[39] In her study of Williamsburg, Winifred Curran shows that gentrification leads to a loss of industrial blue-collar work. T. William Lester and Daniel Hartley argue that gentrification plays a part in accelerating the change from production of goods to the service sector, and Rachel Meltzer and Pooya Ghorbani find that while gentrifying neighborhoods experience a growth in employment opportunities, longtime residents actually lose jobs in their own Census tracts.[40] In examining amenity migration, Neil Argent and colleagues find that the creative class in Australia is attracted to high-amenity rural areas, but there is no association with employment creation.[41]

Yet there is still limited empirical research into the specific ways that gentrification affects employment opportunities for longtime community residents and little focus on seasonal gentrification and its influence on employment, resident perceptions, and quality of life. In this book, we explore how seasonal gentrification has specific compounding effects that may not be seen in other gentrifying communities, particularly when it comes to quality-of-life issues and the lives of children. The current gap in the literature makes it difficult to develop effective employment and training policies in seasonally gentrifying cities and to create housing and development policies that fully benefit these local residents. In the following chapters, we address this gap and contribute to the scholarship on gentrification, race, intersectionality, and employment.

Our Ethnographic Journey

We chose to investigate the New Jersey Shore town of Asbury Park to better understand the connection between jobs and gentrification, specifically in a community that is experiencing seasonal gentrification. This small, 1.6-square-mile seaside city in the New York metropolitan area provides an ideal case study. Asbury Park's history—in terms of both economic development and race relations—makes it a particularly interesting context in which to examine gentrification and employment.

It is with this lens that we developed our study. This book represents a multiyear, multimethod project exploring the impacts of seasonal gentrification on workforce opportunities and lived experiences for the residents in Asbury Park. Over the course of three years (2016–2019), we conducted in-depth interviews, focus groups, and observational research in Asbury Park.[42] Participants (N = 81) included eighteen community activists or educators involved in the West Side of Asbury Park, thirty-four workers (or potential workers) from the West Side community of Asbury Park, thirteen Asbury Park employers (including developers and small business owners), four government representatives, three tourists / former residents, and nine seasonal employees working on the East Side. All the employers, save one, were White. Of the thirty-four workers from the West Side, only one identified as White-alone, and the rest identified as people of color. The community activists were half White and half individuals of color. All interviews and focus groups were recorded (when permission was granted) and transcribed and double-coded (separately by each of us).

In addition to interviews and focus groups, we spent countless hours participating in ethnographic observations of Asbury Park life. We ate at restaurants, stayed at hotels, listened to music at concerts, attended conventions and festivals and rallies, sunbathed at the beaches, attended meetings of city government, and walked throughout the East and West Sides. We had many formal and informal conversations with city officials, residents, workers, and tourists. Both of us came to this project with prior experiences in Asbury Park. Like so many ethnographers before us, our interest in the city stemmed in part from our time in, and knowledge of, the city. Mary Gatta lives about fifteen minutes from Asbury Park and has witnessed its seasonal gentrification over time. She was able to build on her own networks and local knowledge as we developed this book. Molly Vollman Makris was herself one of the many visitors from North Jersey drawn to the beach and community in Asbury Park, and she was able to use her New York City / North Jersey network to help us delve into that perspective. Yet we are not community residents, and as White middle-class professionals, we acknowledge our positionality and privilege and outsider status in Asbury—and in particular on the West Side. For this reason, we rely heavily on the voices of Asbury Park residents throughout this monograph. It was always apparent to us that the true experts would be the people of Asbury Park, New Jersey. One exchange from a focus group with West Side residents perfectly demonstrates the expertise of the community in comparison to our research background:

FACILITATOR: I mean, there's a lot of research that supports exactly what you're saying, that there's a lot of racism and segregation in the—
PARTICIPANT: We ain't got no research. I'm telling you from experience.

We concluded our research when data saturation was reached and then triangulated our findings with more in-depth Census data analysis and respondent validation. We worked with quantitative data consultant Shawn McMahon to analyze U.S. Census, ACS, Consumer Financial Protection Bureau, and Zillow Group Inc. data. After finishing our initial analysis, we also looked closely at the work of Alicia Raia-Hawrylak on children and their parents in Asbury Park and the article "Revitalization Greetings from Asbury Park" by Chris Pomorski, which triangulated our findings.[43] This book is, as far as we know, the only in-depth ethnographic study of a seasonally gentrifying city and the phenomenon's impact at the local level.

Shining Light on All of Dark City

To share our journey into Asbury Park, we have organized this book in a way that details the richness of our interviews and participant observation while ensuring that the stories are grounded in critical sociological frameworks and analysis. We begin by chronicling the history of Asbury Park, nicknamed the Dark City, with a keen racial lens in order to highlight how inequality and anti-Black racism were embedded in the city from the start. We then share the lived experiences of the workers, residents, visitors, business owners, and clients along with our own observations in order to reveal what is occurring every day. Lastly, we highlight a path forward to ensure that residents like the ones we encountered have access to good jobs and economic opportunity.

In chapter 2, "Racial Segregation, Sex, Gender, and Rock 'n' Roll: The History of Asbury Park," we use an intersectional lens as we briefly trace the past in Asbury Park, demonstrating how the racial inequality that was evident in the founding and economic development of the city is reverberating a century later as Asbury Park undergoes seasonal gentrification. We highlight the city's history as a vacation spot since the nineteenth century and its history of music (and more recent associations with rock 'n' roll stars such as Bruce Springsteen). The popular story of decline and renaissance in Asbury Park obscures the experiences of longtime residents who have remained in the community. We also trace the history of Asbury Park's reputation as an LGBTQ-friendly community. We examine the importance of this population to the community and its role in gentrification as well as the perils the LGBTQ community may face as the city changes.

In chapter 3, "Working While Black," we draw on our ethnographic data to discuss the lived experiences of Black and Latino West Side residents who attempt to find work but face many barriers. A companion to chapter 4, here we highlight the challenges that residents of color face in securing work within and around Asbury Park. Issues such as limited types of employment, transportation barriers, information barriers, and criminal records make this process difficult. Here we highlight how spatial, racial, and age mismatch play significant roles in securing and maintaining work and also the treatment of workers. We examine how different racial/ethnic groups perceive their own and others' roles in the economy (e.g., that of Latino workers), and we describe who *is* working on the East Side using an intersectional lens.

Chapter 4, "Owning a Business: The Employers' Side," features two case studies of operations in Asbury Park that are working to improve employment opportunities for longtime residents, the Kula Café and the Salt School. These two organizations have some important similarities and differences. We examine their intentions, struggles, and successes. We then go on to share the stories of the small business owners on the East Side of Asbury Park and their intentions, struggles, and successes more broadly. We highlight their understandings of the economic development in the town, their experiences hiring workers from the West Side, their goals and visions for the town, and how their experiences and beliefs fit into the larger story and challenges of workforce development.

Chapter 5, "A West Side Story," paints a rich picture of what it is like to live on the West Side of Asbury Park while the East Side prospers. We share the stories and the words of residents and educators while looking specifically at issues particular to a seasonally gentrifying community. The themes that arise from our research concern beach access and swimming, amenities, relationships with law enforcement, educational challenges, and community support for children and families. We examine how the history and ongoing racial tensions in Asbury Park and the seasonal gentrification now occurring affect each of these areas. We conclude with the story of Elijah, an in-depth case study of the experiences of one young man coming of age on the West Side, and how his story is representative of so many of the themes throughout the book.

In chapter 6, "Cats Are the New Dogs (and Other Stuff That Makes Asbury Cool . . . and Can It Stay Cool?)," we explore the question, "Why do people come here?" Using our ethnographic data along with analysis of media pieces on Asbury Park, we explore the current fashion industry, art galleries, tattooed-cool vibe, festivals, and cat conventions that are drawing visitors and residents. We contrast this "Cool Asbury," where a tourist can snuggle a cat and purchase a Catsbury Park Springsteen T-shirt, with the experiences of long-term residents of color who are often excluded from this side of Asbury Park. We also look at the increasing role of big developers and the real estate industry in feeding on Asbury's newfound cool and the commodification of diversity. We then ask the question, "Will all this be both figuratively and literally whitewashed away?"

Chapter 7, "Land of Hope and Dreams?," explores our conclusions and policy implications. Present-day Asbury Park represents the nexus of seasonal gentrification, jobs, and intersectionality. In this final chapter, we build on our data and our conversations with community leaders to suggest a path forward that will help ensure a fairer economy and better quality of life for all city residents.

With this book, we hope to advocate for plans that do justice to all members of the community, honor the past, shed light on systemic inequality, and acknowledge the current divide. As one small business owner on the West Side puts it, "There is a huge divide in this town. It [is] literally the west side of the tracks out here, so I would say that it isn't a great feeling to see that . . . there's obviously some development in some areas and some not. So I think even just dealing with kind of the difficulties of that and figuring out a solution to how to kind of make a healthy development rather than just like a displacement [is needed]."

2

Racial Segregation, Sex, Gender, and Rock 'n' Roll

The History of Asbury Park

But they said it was like that back in the day before, though. They kept all us over here, and you couldn't even go across the tracks. I heard that you couldn't do anything, so that's coming back definitely because they're doing everything across the tracks, everything. . . . They say history repeats itself, right?

—West Side resident focus group

We don't want history to forget that Asbury Park is an LGBT community, and we want people that come here to expect the rainbow flags.

—interview, Christian Fuscarino

The music scene in Asbury Park did not start with Bruce Springsteen; there was a vibrant music scene on the West Side going back to the 1930s, '40s, and beyond.

—interview, Yvonne Clayton

Asbury Park's history is complex and multifaceted. In this chapter, we briefly trace the key themes using an intersectional lens in order to uncover the roots of the seasonal gentrification that is now occurring. Asbury Park is infamous for its music scene and the often-referenced *Greetings from Asbury Park* album by Bruce

Springsteen. Bruce has been known to surprise patrons to watch a Giants game or dance with his mom at a local bar.[1] Asbury Park is also well known as an LGBTQ-friendly community where rainbow flags fly proudly on the ocean breeze. The LGBTQ community is simultaneously credited and blamed for the changes that occurred in Asbury in the twenty-first century. But there is a deeper, more complex history behind the music scene and displays of LBGTQ pride. Music in Asbury did not begin with Bruce's album in 1973, and the LGBTQ community was present long before the *New York Times* was covering this alleged renaissance.

As is often the case in gentrifying cities, the contributions of longtime residents and the full history become lost as the media paints a simple picture of a so-called discovery or renaissance. There is a rich dynamic in Asbury Park, where a vibrant Haitian community exists alongside a growing Latino community and African American population, an active LGBTQ community, artists who found a home for their creativity in this town, and an ever-increasing number of wealthy visitors and property owners from New York City, North Jersey, and beyond.

These groups do not, of course, exist in isolation. There are ever-present intersecting identities—Latino artists, Haitians who identify as LGBTQ, wealthy Black tourists, and so on—that must be considered to avoid oversimplification in analyzing the past, present, and future of the city. As one local activist in a focus group mentions, there are within-group differences that must be recognized: "We have class differences in the Black community . . . nobody wants to deal with that." The theory of intersectionality, which looks at marginalized persons in power structures, posits that within groups that share a common identity, there are still differences in gender, race, class, sexuality, religion, or other aspects of one's experience.[2] Stemming from studies of feminism and Black female exclusion from the movement, intersectionality has become a more broadly used concept that is particularly fitting for our examination of Asbury Park. This book provides insight into intersectionality as it plays out in the real world.

The anti-Black racism evident in the early history of Asbury Park is reverberating a century later as the city undergoes seasonal gentrification, particularly in regard to opportunities for jobs in the changing local labor market. There are incredibly complex intersectional dynamics in Asbury Park around race, gender, income, and sexuality. The LGBTQ population is both blamed for gentrification and a potential victim of gentrification itself. LGBTQ persons of color face compound discrimination. Some in the Latino community are suffering under fear of immigration issues in the current political climate and struggling for employment while also being blamed by other socioeconomically disadvantaged people of color for taking jobs and working for little pay. As one focus group participant states, "I'm surrounded by twenty Mexican people, and I have to compete against them every single day. How do they get this work and I don't get it?" A member of the Haitian community calls out the preferences given to Latino parents because communications to families are translated exclusively in Spanish in the schools. Meanwhile, a small business owner tells us of an employee, "She's Latina, and she left town because she felt threatened by the African American people, and that's a problem," and a resident in our Latinx focus group states of these same tensions, "It's just . . . 'cause I guess we're in a Black community, so it's like, they swear they own Asbury, and, like, us Hispanics are I guess intimidated, and [members of the Black community are] always starting a fight and everything." As an LGBTQ resident explains, there is also tension between the Black and LGBTQ communities, and the Black community argues of gay discrimination, "You could pass [as straight]," as opposed to people of color, who likely cannot pass as White.

Early Asbury

The intersectional discussion of this current vacation destination and the urban development of Asbury Park cannot be discussed without beginning with an examination of its history, with race at the forefront. Asbury Park, founded in 1871 by a Methodist named James A. Bradley and named for Bishop Francis Asbury, was reliant on segregation from the start. Historically, the hospitality venues that Asbury Park was known for were staffed by Black men and women who worked as hotelmen, laundresses, waiters, and janitors. Black men were employed pushing rolling wicker carts carrying White tourists up and down the boardwalk.[3] Although they were employed throughout the bustling town, they were not integrated into city life. As historian David Goldberg notes, many Black men and women came to Asbury Park for employment opportunities yet found themselves living separately from the White residents and tourists.[4] A second community of Black residents and other working-class citizens had settled in a community known as the "West End." This area was, according to Bradley's wishes and rooted in his desire to maintain property values, not officially part of the city until it was annexed in 1906 for increased tax revenues.[5]

Racism in Asbury Park was ever present. While White tourists "accepted the presence of African-Americans as members of the working service class, they persistently objected to sitting next to them on trains, lounging alongside them in the surf, and watching the men flirt with white women."[6] As a result, White tourists and residents began pressuring Bradley to segregate the town's public spaces—including the beaches, boardwalk, pavilions, and hotels. Segregation was embedded within the policies Bradley used to guide the economic development of the city itself.

Like racial segregation in nearby Atlantic City, New Jersey, Asbury's founder and its White residents promoted their own northern version of Jim Crow laws. Building on Bryant Simon's analysis of Atlantic City, Goldberg states that many White residents and tourists "objected to legal, southern-style segregation, except when it came to public space—their public spaces—they demanded seclusion."[7] By 1887, Bradley officially restricted all African Americans, both those who worked as well as those who sought to vacation in Asbury Park, from the beaches and other shore facilities by posting signs and positioning officers throughout the town. Chris Pomorski describes the legacy of this in Asbury Park: "A friendly port to the Ku Klux Klan in the '20s, its beaches remained de facto segregated into the '70s."

Yvonne Clayton, an African American Asbury Park council member (who grew up in the city), describes segregation's enduring legacy. She says that as a child, she went to the beach every day—not in Asbury but in Belmar because Belmar was more accepting, and beaches in her hometown had been segregated. She explains, "For my parents, that was stuck in their memory. I don't know anyone who went to the beach in Asbury from the West Side; my mom would drop us off in the morning and come back and pick us up or we would take the bus back." She describes a pool in Asbury but said she never went into it. She explains that in Asbury, there were always certain types of jobs available for young people from her background, but she "never tried to get a summer job on the boardwalk." She declares, "Why bother? A teenager of color?" Instead, she worked in a factory and then in a shoe store on Main Street.

Asbury's musical legacy is also integral to the city's history. As Eileen Chapman, an Asbury Park council member and music expert, explains, there has "always been a music scene in Asbury. When the boardwalk was first developed, there were music pavilions where concert bands and ragtime bands performed, opera in the Paramount Theater, organ recitals in [the] convention hall, and music in all the hotels. Music was always part of what the city provided." She continues, "Along Springwood Avenue, you'd find music by African American performers. Because they were not welcomed in the hotels on the East Side [of] the city, they stayed and performed in small hotels on the West Side." Charlie Horner, a music historian, notes that Asbury Park provided a unique opportunity for musicians as a stop in between Atlantic City and Harlem. Count Basie played Asbury Park, and Duke Ellington spent the summer there as a teenager. Clubs on Springwood Avenue featured the sounds of jazz, gospel, and rhythm and blues. As the city and the nation were experiencing the social and political turmoil of the 1960s, music provided hope. As the

Asbury Park Press, the area's leading newspaper, reports, "In 1968, Asbury Park was the music capital of the Jersey Shore. A 'Summer of Stars' paraded into its venues that summer with acts like The Doors, The Beach Boys, Ray Charles and others jamming out in the city that had live entertainment etched into its soul."[8]

The West Side was not entirely Black, as Chapman explains: "It used to be a real mix on the West Side, including Italian and Jewish and Black populations—a real mix of people who lived and worked harmoniously together." Yet racial segregation was still a steadfast structural factor in the town. In the mid-twentieth century, when the beaches were still divided, more and more White residents were abandoning Asbury Park for affluent suburbs and farther-flung beach vacations (thanks to more accessible air travel), and jobs were beginning to disappear, minority residents increasingly felt that they had been left out of the prosperity that others in the city had enjoyed. By the early 1970s, the music scene (and teen clubs in particular) was well established, but town demographics were shifting, and tourism was decreasing.

At the beginning of the 1970s, Asbury Park's population of seventeen thousand residents was 30 percent Black (the population rose to eighty thousand with summer vacationers). Jobs on the waterfront were increasingly going to young White people from nearby towns, and Black residents were angry about the lack of employment and bad housing conditions.[9] From July 4 to July 10, 1970, tensions and resentment in the community boiled over into a disturbance that destroyed around five blocks of the city's West Side. Over 180 people, including state troopers, were injured, and a dusk-to-dawn curfew was temporarily imposed. Damages were estimated at $4 million, and $1.6 million was required for cleanup.

As Clayton explains, "There were factories [back then] where people could work. Many of my classmates worked there. And when they started to close and malls opened and those [factory] jobs went away, what that did to the West Side was devastating, including the civil disobedience of the '70s. . . . Springwood Avenue employed a large number of the community. Everything you needed could be found there: a butcher, a department store, record stores, an electrician, pharmacies, restaurants, and nightclubs." As in many other cities, fallout from the disturbances further exacerbated an already bad economic situation. According to the *New York Times*, in Asbury Park, there were 10,000 hotel and motel rooms in 1966. By 1976, there were fewer than 1,500. In the 1980s, even the *Asbury Park Press* moved its operations to the suburbs (where it remains to this day).

As businesses and residents left, Asbury Park's reputation as a popular resort destination suffered. The once-thriving boardwalk was in desperate need of investors. The city's two vintage carousels were sold and shipped out of state. The jazz and rock clubs were slowly disappearing. The city struggled with violence, drugs, prostitution, and homelessness as well as significant corruption within the police department, the schools, and the city government. By the end of the twentieth century, Asbury Park was perceived by some as a dangerous ghost town, even being referred to as "Beirut on the Jersey Shore."[10] During our research, we heard *many* stories about the "old Asbury Park." People from other parts of New York and New Jersey would tell us their tales of braving the "dangerous" streets of Asbury Park to attend concerts or enjoy the scene at raves under a bridge or that they simply steered clear of Asbury altogether.

"The People of Asbury Park Never Went Away"

In a review of Asbury Park's history, it is too easy to overlook this key period. All too often, there is an oversimplification of the era of disinvestment in cities. For many, Asbury was falsely perceived as a ghost town or a town of pure vice. However, during this time, there were generations of city residents who attended schools, fell in love, had successful careers in Asbury or elsewhere, and raised children—some of whom stayed in the community and some who did not. There were business owners who managed to maintain businesses in the city despite the fact that government policies nationally were disinvesting in urban infrastructure and favoring suburban growth. There were families that *had* a choice and *chose* Asbury Park. There were LGBTQ individuals who found a safe haven in the gay bars of Asbury Park long before others took note of this.

Residents we interviewed do not have wholly negative memories of this era. Many middle-aged West Side residents remember fondly running barefoot through the Asbury Park of their youth:

PARTICIPANT 1: Remember when we used to run down to the beach barefooted . . .
PARTICIPANT 2: Playing and . . .
PARTICIPANT 1: The quietness.

They wistfully describe living on the West Side before they felt it fully changed. They describe a West Side where residents looked out for one another and children had many more resources and activities. One activist declares,

> The success of the West Side was when this strip right here had businesses that prospered. Everything—clothing stores, shoe stores—I mean everything we wanted we had on this side of town, so we can get up, go to a grocery store. It was no problem, and it was actually when you can actually walk to a grocery store and say, "Look, my mom said give her a pound of bologna, a loaf of bread," and the guy would write it on a piece of paper . . . and you'd go back on Friday and you'd pay him, and that's it because it was a tight sense of community.

As one resident in a West Side focus group explains about the changes she has seen,

> We had the boardwalk. I mean, you could go down to the boardwalk and stay down there all day and ride the rides. I mean, [now] they don't have anything—nowhere around here. The West Side community, they done moved everybody from the outside in

there now. There are no buses coming in, and most of the kids are not getting in—you know, the places like after school programs, you know? They took everything; you know what I'm saying?

A Haitian American woman with an advanced degree who has settled outside of Asbury Park but was raised on the East Side of the city during this era reflects on how those who lived in Asbury during this time are often forgotten:

I do not appreciate how the people who have stayed are being treated. I do not appreciate the narrative that it is something new. The people of Asbury Park never went away. Even when the beaches were full of trash, I went with my friends and cleared spots to sit and enjoy the ocean. "Oh, Asbury Park is making a comeback." We were always there; we stayed. I still called it my beach and still called it home. Even when it was filled with crack vials and trash and people turned up their noses, I went to Asbury Park. There is now a displacement of people who did stay when those changes were happening, and I don't know where they've gone. It is no longer affordable even for me, who grew up in Asbury Park. I am outpriced; I can't purchase a home in Asbury Park.

An LGBTQ community member shared this sentiment: "The newbies like to say, 'Oh my God! Asbury was so horrible!' They are New Yorkers—from the Hamptons."

We heard how shifts in retail influenced the community. For instance, places like Woolworths Department Store served to connect the West and East Sides, and in today's Asbury, this does not exist. A small business owner pointed out that even after Asbury Park lost its long-standing retail establishments like Woolworths and Steinbach department stores, all was not abandoned, and to say so undermines those that were there: "Relatively new people talk about [how] when they got here, there were tumbleweeds going down Cookman [a commercial thoroughfare]. Well, that's a load of crap, you know. I bought my house here in 2000, and Cookman was deserted. No question about it. But there were *still* businesses there. Mr. Fashion was there. There were businesses there."

LGBTQ residents told us stories of finding a welcoming place during this era in Asbury. Gay and lesbian bars that catered to their community opened during this time of disinvestment. "There were a few gay bars here in [the] 1970s in little hidden spots," one LGBTQ bar owner explains. "We rented the space [for our bar]—a tiny space, we were broke. When it got cold and we couldn't keep up with oil, we broke up furniture and burned it in the fireplace for heat. . . . At that time, there were quite a few straight bars, there were a few Black bars. But the amazing thing was that in 1979 and 1980, we had no problems with gays and straights; we were a melting pot."

During this period, there was still a division between the East and West Sides, but the extreme wealth and influx of White residents of today's Asbury were not yet factors, and the earlier tourist wealth had fled. The Haitian American woman who grew up on the East Side touches on this intersectionality in the community and reminisces about her childhood in the 1980s:

> Growing up, all I remember is having fun. I could see Tilly
> [a nickname for a locally infamous figure from an amusement
> park mural] from my house. I would play with kids from the
> local blocks—play tag and hide-and-seek and walk to the beach
> together, just hang out and sit on the porch and tell jokes. Late
> at night, sit on the porch and be so silly. Sit on the roof and the
> kids across the street on their roof. African American, Haitian,
> Latino—not a significant White population, but there were
> White kids. Maybe about five White friends. . . . You would hear
> that is where the drug dealers live, on the West Side—don't go
> there because it is not safe. Don't go there, be careful, the police
> are always there. Not so much your safety but the "wrong kids"
> sort of thing. . . . [There was a] sense of elitism about which
> side of town you were from. Not really a racial divide because
> we were all people of color. But there was a divide that did exist.

Actually, in the '80s, unfortunately, [there was] the narrative in the news, and African Americans were not very nice to Haitians. There was discriminatory behavior toward Haitians "boat people," and [people were] saying, "Haitians bringing AIDS to America" or are "off the boat." But as a Haitian, I was very proud to be Haitian, but Haitian kids were teased.

She then explains how policing in that era felt different than it does now with the racial divide gentrification has created:

There's a change in policing. Growing up, the police were community minded. As an African American child of color, I never had a bad experience. I remember the police playing with us and giving us rides home to make sure we got home safely. Teasing [Officer] "Mike Mike" and him giving us advice about boys. Him telling our parents not to discipline us. And this was a White man. That is the memory I have. Now [2018] I don't have that level of respect because I see how they treat people of color, and they treat us as if we don't belong. My nephews and my brothers get harassed.

An LGBTQ resident who worked in gay bars of this era expresses a similar sentiment: "Back then, police officers would walk you to your car because there were some bad folks out there. We as a community stuck together. The cops were great."

This was also a period when, despite the many jazz and soul clubs closing and the convention hall losing its luster, music still flourished in Asbury Park. According to journalist Austin Bogues, "Springsteen rose to bigger national prominence even as the city faded."[11] In fact, Bruce Springsteen has said he chose the title of his debut album, *Greetings from Asbury Park*, because it made clear his connection to the city and New Jersey as opposed to New York City. As Councilwoman Chapman explains, "As the larger hotels closed, nightclubs popped up on the East Side." Venues such as the Fast Lane, Rainbow Room, M&K, and the Stone Pony opened their doors during this time of supposed urban decay. Chapman says, "All of those places provided many different types of entertainment, and there was an audience for every genre of music . . . everyone did things differently in order to survive." Music was often a reason for visiting Asbury when nothing else was drawing people in. In 1981, U2 played two shows at the Fast Lane, and a young Jon Bon Jovi got his start there in high school.[12] Places like Asbury Lanes became infamous alternative rock venues in the early 2000s.

Gaytrification

In the early 2000s, the town began to experience changes. Gay men and lesbians gravitated to Asbury Park as a less expensive beach destination than Fire Island and the Hamptons. Many young professionals from New York City and northern New Jersey came to Asbury Park via train. The city's abandoned buildings were ripe for development. In the northwest section of town, those looking for fixer-uppers quickly bought old Victorian homes. Asbury Park was quickly becoming a summer vacation destination once again.

Gaytrification has been used to describe phenomena like that which occurred in Asbury Park. David Christafore and Susane Leguizamon find that "areas with more same-sex coupled households did, indeed, have a higher predicted probability of gentrifying from 2000 to 2010. A 1 percentage point increase in the number of same-sex coupled households is associated with an almost 2% to 3% increase in the probability of gentrification."[13]

However, it is important to recognize that Asbury provided a place for the LGBTQ community long before the start of the new millennium. LGBTQ history cannot be separated from Asbury's history or said to "start" at a certain moment in time. In the 1800s, LGBTQ people escaped to the boardwalks of the Jersey Shore to have a good time, and Asbury Park has always been a cultural hub for this population. The LGBTQ community was more closeted at that time, and as such, there is little formal documentation. As one LGBTQ resident explains, "Any place where there are bars or gathering spots with upstairs or backroom spaces, you can bet

LGBT people were there." In the 1950s and '60s, Asbury Park likely had an LGBTQ community that was similar to the one on Fire Island. Folks like Judy Garland were said to have vacationed with LGBTQ friends and stayed in Asbury Park at the Empress and Berkeley Carteret.[14] Asbury, Long Branch, and Atlantic City were seen as the "three pillars on the shore" that provided an alternative to Fire Island. As one NJ.com article states, "Gays in the Garden State have long congregated in towns like Jersey City, Plainfield, Asbury Park and Collingswood, but have mostly lived their lives in more low-key fashion."[15] One lesbian former resident of Asbury Park states that when she wanted to move to New Jersey in 1975, "Asbury Park seemed like one of only two places that would be open to a gay couple."

We were told by local LGBTQ residents that in the 1980s, Asbury Park had ten to twelve gay bars. One activist remembers, "Bond Street used to be [a] lesbian bar—you would knock, and there was a peephole, and they would verify you were a lesbian and let you in." Another explains, "Asbury Park was known widely as a space where LGBT people were occupying. In the '70s and '80s, it was known for that, but even in the 1800s they came here." As one LGBTQ business owner explains, "That's how gay bars thrive: we find a rundown city or part of a city, we come in, we take over, and [we] plant a flower and get the roof done. The gays in Asbury kept the city thriving and moving." The rainbow flag, so commonly seen in Asbury today, represented more than just pride to the residents of that time. As we were told by an LGBTQ activist, "When AIDS hit, a rainbow flag was your safe haven, and people would take care of you."

Thus when the public narrative only mentions LGBTQ persons in Asbury at the start of the new millennium, it ignores their long history in the community. Prior to the 1990s, LGBTQ establishments fulfilled an incredibly powerful function in the gay community. LGBTQ individuals from Pennsylvania and New Jersey all found refuge in Asbury. As one activist explains, "Asbury Park's LGBT history until the 2000s is really only found in the bars. There were no great societies meeting here; the bar scene has been the place for the LGBTQ community to find a safe haven. These LGBT establishments, like others in cities, were paying off police not to raid." For many, gay bars represent a first place of acceptance. Many of these establishments on the East Coast were controlled by the mafia, who would pay off the police to stay in business. The Stonewall riots famously began in one such bar in Greenwich Village, New York, in 1969. These were places where gay men and lesbians gathered together and then came up against the forces of the law and discrimination.[16]

In 1999, music producer Robert "Shep" Pettibone (coproducer of Madonna's "Vogue") opened the gay club Paradise in Asbury Park, which he still owns. Paradise is now alleged to be the oldest continuously operating gay club in New Jersey. One longtime patron explains the club's importance in the LGBTQ community: "We needed it. . . . It was someplace where you didn't have to worry about somebody outing you."[17] Yet Pettibone's enterprise here also signaled a shift in the community in terms of investment.

Thus the sea change in the LGBTQ community and in Asbury Park occurred not when gays "started arriving" but when LGBTQ residents from New York City and North Jersey started investing in property. The activist we interviewed about this feels that the '90s were a transition period that paved the way for the attractiveness of the Asbury community to outsiders: "The '90s were a more mature version of the '70s and '80s. The population just grew up and wanted homes, not just bars—and that is what attracted the North Jersey and NYC money. The AIDS crisis matured people, and many died. Those who survived took life seriously—we've been given this gift of life—take this seriously. . . . The '90s were 'We made it through.' Early 2000s, the money was coming in . . . that's really when you see the divide begin." Another LGBTQ community member expresses a similar sentiment: "From the mid-1990s to the bubble burst is when the rich LGBTQ came in." He tells us that people would say, "Here comes more money than God . . . here comes the heterosexuals." In many ways, these changes in Asbury Park mirror the postrecession gentrification process that

occurred in the late 1990s in New York City, with a heavy helping hand from corporate developers and the state.[18] Kathe Newman and Elvin Wyly illustrate this shift as seen by residents in
Central Harlem: "The changes during the late 1990s and early
2000s are different. Harlem's residents report a solid flow of SUVs
(sports utility vehicles) of people driving through the neighborhood scouting for homes."[19]

During our research in Asbury, we would hear residents, particularly those of color, blame LGBTQ residents for gentrification.
While this connection (e.g., gaytrification) cannot be denied, it is
complex. One LGBTQ community member explains their affilia-
tion with an Asbury Park marketing fund: "We took gay dollars
and tried to get people to look at Asbury—we would advertise in
the mid-1990's, looking for the Fire Island crowd." Yet currently,
LGBTQ activists are concerned about their own displacement. As
Christian Fuscarino of Garden State Equality states, "I'm worried
about the LGBT population being pushed out by folks from more
wealthy areas who want this to be their summer home. The wealthy
LGBT couples that live here are more likely to invest in the local
community than a couple that has no connection to the culture."

In 2004, "a decade before the New Jersey Supreme Court ruled
in favor of marriage equality," the then deputy mayor of Asbury
Park married a gay couple at city hall, marking "the first same-
gender marriage in New Jersey, and among the first in the nation."[20]
Today in Asbury and elsewhere, Fuscarino explains, "There's a
pride section at Target and six-year-olds who can articulate their
transgender experience." During Pride Month, mainstream establishments from Dunkin' Donuts to Eddie Bauer to Colgate celebrate pride. Of this shift, one gay Asbury resident remarks,

It's bittersweet. It's a different era. It's a different mind-set. I'm
forty-one. I love going to Paradise, I hate going to Paradise. Now
it's overthrown by bachelorette parties. I want to kill someone,
you know? And that's a good thing. It's sweet. They don't know
the struggle. They never had issues with coming out or gay

bashing or anything. That's a fantastic thing, but they will go to Watermark [restaurant], and they will go to this place and feel comfortable, and that's a fantastic thing. Our older crowd is a little bit different . . . so I could see how on the horizon, that's a really wonderful thing, but also it's kind of like, "God, I just want my space back!" . . . But progress is good, and like I said earlier . . . with change comes . . . acceptance and everything else.

With this shift, the role of bars in the gay community has also shifted (we heard about the invasion of bachelorette parties into gay bars more than once), and there is not an expansion of gay bars in Asbury because traditionally straight spaces are now more accepting.

Yet intersectionality is at play, and many LGBTQ people in Asbury are negatively impacted by the very gentrification they are so often blamed for. Their relationships with the West Side and longtime residents of color are complicated. The LGBTQ community has provided a welcome home for LGBTQ West Side residents and their allies, but they are also seen invaders and face discrimination themselves. One LGBTQ community member divulges, "I have a friend renting a house on [the West Side]. He hung his flag up, he plants perennials and is planting tomato plants, he painted the garage, he's having a Corona, and someone pulls up [and says,] 'I can't believe you fucking faggots are taking over here. First the beach, and now over here.' [The West Side residents are] still feeling a hidden agenda, and that is not it."

Another LGBTQ resident laments, "I'm worried that the gays who kept this city together are going to get pushed out." LGBTQ people of color experience a much higher rate of poverty than straight people of color. LGBTQ youth of color are kicked out of their homes at higher rates and have less support from their parents. In fact, according to a national survey of service providers, LGBTQ youth comprise 40 percent of those served by the organizations sampled.[21] In Asbury, trans women of color are particularly impacted by gentrification. Straight people of color have other communities of support when they are displaced, but trans people of color may not be able to find other groups that accept them. As Fuscarino points out, gentrification "has impacted the LGBTQ population in ways probably larger than any other community. [For example,] a large percentage of sex workers are transgender. When outsiders come in and pressure law enforcement to crack down on those types of activities, sex workers no longer have a source of income."

Other well-known traditionally gay communities, nicknamed "gayborhoods," such as Greenwich Village and the Castro District, are struggling with demographic shifts, or "straightening." These gayborhoods, once seen as necessities, are now perceived as less essential as gay individuals and families begin to have more political power and support. According to Amin Ghaziani, these neighborhoods appeared in cities during World War II, when those suspected of homosexuality were discharged from the armed forces. Amenities sprang up to support this displaced community, leading to what Kath Weston calls the "Great Gay Migration" to big cities.[22] Today, economic factors are also impacting these gayborhoods. They have become incredibly desirable and expensive places to live. In Seattle's traditionally gay Capitol Hill community, the tech sector has pushed out the gay community, and its new residents tend to be "heavily straight and heavily male," according to local artist John Criscitello, who describes the neighborhood as now "a puke-and-leave drinking destination."[23]

LGBTQ people still do face discrimination and violence despite societal shifts, and now in Asbury Park, they are also faced with the threat of displacement and the loss of their cultural identity. As Fuscarino explains, the *New York Times* might credit the LGBTQ population with the changes in Asbury, and he recognizes the ways in which that is problematic and coded, but he also thinks it is a positive thing: "I don't want history to forget that this is an LGBT community, and I want people to expect the rainbow flags." It is important to this community that it remains, as one LGBTQ resident says, "the unofficial gay capital of New Jersey." However,

FIG. 9. House with a rainbow flag. Photograph by Erika Bentley Leonard, September 10, 2019.

LGBTQ persons still feel unsure of what the future could hold. As illustrated by one of our interviewees, "We still have reason to worry in the Trump years. You don't want to lose safe havens in case you need them."

Current Divisions

As the new millennium ushered in changes to Asbury Park, the old community divisions remained and were exacerbated by seasonal gentrification and informed by intersectionality. The *Asbury Park Press* noted in 2014, "To the east, a blooming waterfront and downtown thrives with summer tourists, bars, eclectic shops, upscale condominiums and a growing gay community. To the west lies an enclave of deteriorating public housing projects, bodegas, rental homes and most of the schools in the city's troubled district. City developers have spent the last decade rebuilding the waterfront, promising the community that West Side redevelopment is next."[24] Clearly, the racial inequality that structured economic, educational, and housing opportunities a century earlier continued to mark the seaside city a century later. As one White community activist explains,

> But you know, when we look at the 140-year history of Asbury Park, it was created by a racist, homophobic guy . . . but anyway, the point being, you know, What does it mean that we live in a city that was created for that [racism] and off the bat wasn't wildly just racist but also classist? You know, Asbury wasn't always Black. You know, in the sixties and seventies, it was heavily Black and amazing and very vibrant, but before, when it was created, it was Black, and there was a lot of working-class White folks as well, and so it's kind of still a similar dynamic. The West Side was created for working-class folks to do the jobs that upper-class, middle-class folks weren't willing to do on the East Side. So just like with that understanding, that's what the city was built for, and that's still what it's doing.

Despite the recent growth of the beach amenities and the downtown area, the economic opportunities in Asbury Park are not equally distributed, and unlike in the past, the service jobs are not overwhelmingly held by West Side residents. Economic development has been significant—twenty-two shops have opened downtown since 2008, and boardwalk businesses generated $30 million in sales in 2014. Waterfront parking fees soared from $0 in 2008 to $1.7 million in 2014.[25] Yet despite the increasing popularity of the community among those with social, cultural, and economic capital, Asbury Park is the poorest city in Monmouth County.

The community is very much divided along the railroad tracks, with the East Side experiencing gentrification. West Side residents are thus feeling left out and nervous about their rapidly changing city and their place within it.

The percentage of people living below the poverty line in Asbury Park in 2017, 30.4 percent, is essentially unchanged since the 2000 Census. Poverty rates west of the tracks, in Census tracts

FIG. 10. West Side stores. Photograph by Molly Vollman Makris, July 25, 2017.

8072 and 8073, are the highest, at 51.4 percent and 34.4 percent, respectively.[26] College completion rates vary widely by group, with 48 percent of White residents holding a bachelor's degree or higher compared to 9.5 percent of Black residents and 11 percent of Hispanic residents.[27] Historically, Asbury Park's unemployment rates are much higher than statewide rates, and the

FIG. 11. Bench on the West Side. Photograph by Erika Bentley Leonard, September 10, 2019.

unemployment rates among African Americans have consistently been 50 percent higher than those among White residents. White residents earn the most, with median annual earnings of $50,667, while African Americans earn the least, with median annual earnings of $21,975.[28] And according to American Community Survey (ACS) estimates, by 2017, Asbury Park residents were 42 percent African American, 30 percent Hispanic/Latino, and 25 percent White.[29] In addition, 23 percent of the population is foreign born, and 32 percent speak a language other than English in the home.[30] Asbury Park High School, the only district high school in the city, is hypersegregated: 98 percent of students identify as Black or Latino, 19 percent have disabilities, and 87 percent are socioeconomically disadvantaged.[31]

The divisions in town are part of why many residents of the West Side feel that their community is not a good place to raise children.

FACILITATOR: Do you think it's still quiet here? I mean, is the quiet something of the past?

FIG. 12. Asbury Park Boardwalk. Photograph by Erika Bentley Leonard, September 10, 2019.

PARTICIPANT 1: No, not at all—not even on this side of town.
PARTICIPANT 2: Not even on this side.
FACILITATOR: So what's the noise on your side [West Side]?
PARTICIPANT 1: Gunshots.
FACILITATOR: Gunshots, the noise on this side of town . . .
PARTICIPANT 2: Gunshots, police cars, and fire cars.
PARTICIPANT 1: They just had a shootout. They just had like a shootout three days in a row.
PARTICIPANT 2: But I don't understand why this police station is here, 'cause they seem to never hear nothing. I don't understand that. Now, we work here, we volunteer, and we hear it.

The daily struggles of West Side residents seem to be especially pronounced against the backdrop of a rapidly seasonally gentrifying East Side. As one activist explains, "That's the problem in this city—that on one side of town, there's a great belief, and on the other side of town, there's like no belief. There's no trust." Others describe their West Side community as being "ignored for the last fifty years." A small business owner warns that the tension generated by this division could erupt:

PARTICIPANT: I mean, and it may not be this summer, but ultimately if the rich get richer and the poor get poorer—if we keep seeing businesses grow in development on the East Side, and [the] West Side doesn't have a dry cleaner, doesn't have a restaurant, doesn't have a bus stop . . .

FACILITATOR: Yes.

PARTICIPANT: Well, this is not going to work.

FACILITATOR: No.

PARTICIPANT: But next time, people—they're not going to only burn the West Side.

FACILITATOR: Right.

PARTICIPANT: They're going to burn everything. And you know, I don't encourage that 'cause nobody wins, but you understand the level of frustration.

Asbury Gentrification

In Asbury Park, the gentrification that in the past felt like a distant possibility is clearly all too real for residents now. The biggest struggle resulting from this shift is the increasing unaffordability of Asbury. On the East Side, where for decades the redevelopment of the boardwalk seemed like it might never happen as developers went bankrupt and the many plans disappeared into thin air, the changes are finally evident. An article on Asbury's gentrification in the *Guardian* states of recent changes, "Developers now own many of the venues most closely associated with the brand of New Jersey quirk that brought Asbury back. For example, the Stone Pony, made famous by Springsteen, is also owned by developers."[32] Today the community is out of reach for the working or middle class. However, one developer we interviewed justifies luxury development in the community: "It takes five $200,000 homes to create the tax revenue of one $1 million home." While in

2003 the *New York Times* pondered the future for Asbury, today the *Times* writes of its "comeback" story with its art gallery, boutique hotel, and vintage shops.[33]

Gentrification in Asbury Park is not limited to new, expensive development on the East Side or to the turnover of once-affordable properties by the beach; the tentacles of gentrification will reach throughout the entire community. Landlords all over the city will increase rents. Residents we spoke to described how this already influences their lives. One participant in a focus group of Latinx individuals recounts,

PARTICIPANT: I was paying $1,200 a month.
FACILITATOR: Uh-huh.
PARTICIPANT: Then my landlord was saying that he's gonna start charging $1,800 a month.
FACILITATOR: Uh-huh.
PARTICIPANT: And I'm like, "Oh, my!" That's $600 more.

A local activist explains, "I could pull out a *triCityNews* from nine months ago [2018], turn to the back pages, and look at the real estate ads, and I can show you properties on the West Side that at that time—older stuff, blue-collar-type housing, single-family detached, probably built in the '40s or '50s that nine months ago was listed between $125 and $150,000. That same house today is being listed for closer to $300 if not over $300,000. So gentrification has become real." And a small business owner describes how these changes have shifted dynamics on the street: "You can go down any of these streets north of Asbury Avenue and west of the rails, which three, four years ago were very—like kind of pocketed little areas of cleaned porches and stuff, but you saw a lot more people hanging out. . . . Now there's a dumpster every other third house being restored, renovated. I bet you don't see people hanging out."

The Census numbers demonstrate this as well, with home-ownership rates falling among residents with some college credits or an associate degree from 30 percent in 2010 to 14 percent in 2017.[34] The proportion of Asbury Park residents who rent has always been high and higher than in neighboring jurisdictions. In 2017, approximately 80 percent of Asbury residents rented their homes, making them susceptible to gentrification in a way that homeowners are not.[35] We hear about Asbury as a gentrifying community with trendy boutiques that attract fashion experts scoping the latest trends, yet there is no affordable grocery store for residents. As the stores become increasingly expensive and cater to a seasonal crowd, longtime residents struggle to obtain basic amenities (this will be discussed in more detail in chapter 6).

Every conversation we had with business owners and activists seemed to shift toward what people do *not* want Asbury to become. One such interviewee declares, "*No!* I don't want it to become Pier Village—none of us want that."[36] These residents express what they love about Asbury, their fears for its future, and the recent positive shifts they have noticed. As local politician Chapman explains, "I wanted my children to live in a diverse and culturally vibrant community, and so I raised my three children here. During the downturn of the city, I'd rarely see a baby carriage in town, but that has since changed, and now Words [book store] is hosting children's events, the Lakehouse is providing music lessons for underserved youth, there are two playgrounds on the beach and one on Springwood, [and] there was recently a program in Sunset Park where local kids learned about wildlife and the lake, and [there are] so many other interactive opportunities for families."

The city is faced with balancing development and capital interest in Asbury with the needs and desires of both longtime and newer residents. Much has been made of the tax abatement, or PILOT (payment in lieu of taxes), agreements in Asbury and in other cities in New Jersey like Hoboken, Jersey City, Atlantic City, and neighboring Long Branch. These agreements, which are used to incentive development in "blighted" areas, are much liked by developers. As Chapman explains, "We feel those PILOTs have run their course unless [there is] some unique opportunity. We recently had a local developer ask for two, and we turned them down. I believe developers are now more confident in investing in

Asbury Park. We're still stuck with those PILOTs that were created a long time ago that definitely affected the budget, but at that time, they were necessary to jump-start the development process."

While all eyes are on the major developers in Asbury Park—iStar Financial and Madison Marquette—smaller property owners will have a huge impact on the future of the community. Out-of-town owners are not particularly connected with the community, and their interests differ from the major developers, who face public scrutiny and media attention. Our participants described having investors and potential owners trying to buy their properties. An activist with an organization on the West Side explains, "These are folks who are coming down and knocking on every door. We've had them knock on our doors about selling properties. That is happening rapidly."

A fight over short-term rentals like Vrbo and Airbnb in Asbury Park brought some of these issues to the forefront. While advocates for the measure to limit short-term rentals said they would allow corporations and investors to profit, change residential communities, increase rents, and decrease housing stock for longtime residents, others argued they hurt property owners with high tax bills or benefited the large hotels at the expense of local homeowners. Deputy mayor Amy Quinn described the measure to stop short-term rentals if a property was not a primary residence (which grandfathered in people who did not stand to benefit financially) as one of the most important policies made in Asbury Park to slow the process of gentrification.

Another ongoing topic of conversation during our fieldwork was the school system, which will be discussed in more detail in chapter 5. Issues regarding schools play into the current state of seasonal gentrification and inequity. Longtime West Side residents with whom we spoke were not happy with the education system. While some residents and those involved with schools touted recent improvements, no one said the school system is highly successful. During our research, we were told on multiple occasions that none of the Asbury Park school board members send their children to the public schools. There is interdistrict choice in neighboring communities, which allows parents with capital to navigate the system to send their children out of the district. There are also now two charter schools, which affect the demographics and budget of district schools and create tension within the community. The very high per-student budget for Asbury district schools was often pointed to—particularly by those who see no need to give more money to what they perceive to be low-functioning institutions. One local activist explains the need to get more students into the high school: "We have like fifty kids graduating; that is a lot of overhead." With a large seasonal population, undercrowded schools, and schools that are already ranked high for funding, the district receives little support for more funding. Also, PILOT agreements, like the waterfront development, mean that no funding from these developments goes to the schools: "The school district gets nothing. This contrasts with a typical tax bill where often 50 percent or more of the total goes to the school district."[37]

Music Monday at Springwood Park

It is a scorching-hot summer night as we make our way back to the West Side for the Monday-night concert series. Today our research has reached deep into both the west side and the east side of town, and at times what we have heard has been so difficult, we are feeling exhausted from the responsibility to do it justice. As we head west, we wonder aloud how the turnout will be for this outdoor concert on such an uncomfortable— over 90 degree—night. The crowd at the concert is not huge, but there are certainly people there—a diverse group spread out on blankets, sitting on benches, and in chairs on the lawn. There is a table set up where you can buy "Music Saved Asbury Park" merchandise. Nearby sit the mayor and two city councilpeople. We walk through the playground area, where a woman who appears disoriented yells at us incomprehensibly and angrily under the din of the singer.

—adapted from field notes, 2018

This concert was more than just a night of live music with a diverse crowd. In June 2016, this new West Side park represented the culmination of twelve years of hard work. At the grand opening, councilwoman Yvonne Clayton shares her excitement with the *Asbury Park Sun*: "When I first moved back to town, the Springwood Avenue of my youth had been long gone. . . . It is my hope is [*sic*] that this park will become a safe haven for children play and a community to gather—not only for the concerts and special events but as a quiet place to go and sit and enjoy nature, a place for parents to bring their children, a place for seniors to go and play cards and talk, a place for everyone to just be outside and enjoy nature."[38]

The Asbury Park Music Foundation administered the Levitt AMP Summer Music Series beginning that same summer. As Councilwoman Chapman tells us, "When we opened the park three years ago, we began hosting a Monday night concert series . . . prior to that [there were] so many different plans for Springwood Avenue that had been drawn up and shelved, so no one trusted it would happen." But happen it did, and in 2016, when the city began hosting concerts on the West Side, she says, "People loved it. It was a reason for people from all corners of the city to come together in one space. Music binds neighborhoods and builds communities."

The grant funding for ten music events had specific criteria that resulted in concerts that, at first, did not feel connected to the community. The following year, the leaders sought out a mix of local musicians as well as bigger names. They wanted every opener to be from the West Side, which presented a challenge, but they turned to the community to help find those artists. In the end, two of the bands also managed foundations that worked with school-aged musicians in town.

Events like this one point to a path forward for Asbury. Importantly, a new park represents not just an investment in the West Side in general but an investment in children and families in a seasonally gentrifying community, as some participants in our focus groups note.

PARTICIPANT 1: The park is real significant, really significant. First, a barren landscape for forty-plus years. Now a beautiful park— the first public park in the city's history on the West Side. But more important than frankly it's physical attribute is that it now represents an asset in a neighborhood where there are very few assets.

The local community has come to embrace the asset in part because of the programming that goes on in the park, the concerts, and the fairs, and the festivals. The local community has embraced it as now an asset within their community, but it's also serving the purpose that is getting the local community, which was frankly and honestly an insular community for a long time—maybe not by their choice but because no one came to the West Side. What became an insular community now comes to understand that because there is a destination point on the West Side, they're getting comfortable with the idea that people from outside the community are now coming to the community . . . it's attracting people to the West Side.

The first concert we had there about three years ago was that first Monday-night concert. There were thirty or forty cars parked across the street. I would have bet my last dollar that every single group that got out of those cars hadn't been to the West Side.

PARTICIPANT 2: Ever, yeah.

PARTICIPANT 1: Ever, and now there's a reason to come to the West Side. So in terms of the evolving aspect of this community, that park is really important, really important. If you could have captured . . . a picture of just the last concert this summer, where it was a beastly hot day. I in fact said at 2:00 in the afternoon, "They need to red flag this concert tonight and move it to another day because no one's going to come." How wrong I could be. There were four or five hundred people in the park that night. The band was terrific. By the time they were into their third or fourth or fifth song, there were two hundred people up dancing. There were Black people dancing with White people. There were uniformed police officers dancing, and there was a smile on every single face in the park that night.

And yet this park does not mean an end to the deep divisions in this community. We heard criticisms from longtime residents that the park is not enough. Some residents are concerned that the organizers and planners have overlooked the children of Asbury: "Springwood Park they made it, but [they are] always having stuff like the jazz festival . . . *no* plan for Asbury Park's future includes our children." Many West Siders and residents of color remain cynical overall. A deacon in town, Daniel Harris, was quoted explaining how the history of Asbury makes it difficult for him to trust that the city will work for the best interests of the West Side. As he puts it, "How many times can you do me dirty, and then say, 'Let's try this again'?"[39]

3

Working While Black

One summer weekend, Molly spends a few days vacationing in Asbury Park. In between time on the beach, she eats three lunches and two dinners amid the famed boardwalk, hotels, and bustling Cookman Avenue. All five of the waiters and waitresses who bring her food, the two bartenders who mix her drinks, and the barista who makes her beverage at a coffeehouse are White men and women aged about twenty-five to forty. They largely share a young, hip self-presentation and are well versed in the cultural capital of serving the growing tourist population. At the hotel, there is a young, attractive White woman serving a specialty cocktail in the lobby and telling guests about the music and entertainment the hotel has booked for the weekend. Asbury's tourist-friendly restaurants and bars, at least in the customer-facing front of the house, tend to be filled with predominately White, young, and middle-class people.

A walk along the Asbury Park Boardwalk on another summer day provides a slightly different window into the labor market of the local community. On one side of the boardwalk, where there is a miniature golf course, a splash pad, psychics, fashionable stores, and restaurants, a number of employees are largely

White middle-class college students from nearby suburban communities like Tinton Falls, Bradley Beach, Ocean Township, and Fair Haven. One of these young White men tells us of his plans to go to medical school after he finishes college, and his coworker, also a young White male, shares that he is studying economics and engages in a conversation with us about his academic and professional interests. They both clearly enjoy this temporary summer opportunity to work on the famous Asbury Park Boardwalk; one says that he "loves it!"

There are also young women and men of color employed on the beaches and boardwalk food stands. One Black female high school student tells us, "There are always jobs." One young man of color says he found his job through his mother's employer. Another young man of color from a local high school is employed checking badges through a summer youth employment program funded by the U.S. Department of Labor. His story provides a window into the larger story of Asbury Park. He has lived in Asbury his entire life and tells us he has a close relative who was displaced due to the recent gentrification in the community.

Our analysis of Census Bureau data highlights the changing labor market for Asbury Park residents, as seen in figure 13. Between 2008 and 2017, Asbury residents' employment notably increased in three industries (defined by the U.S. Department of Labor): retail trades (3.6 percentage points); arts, entertainment, recreation, accommodation, and food services (3.4 percentage points); and professional, scientific, management, and administrative services (3.0 percentage points). In fact, employment in arts, entertainment, recreation, accommodation, and food services rose in Asbury while it decreased in neighboring shore towns. However, it is important to note that these industries do not represent the largest share of employment: the education, health care, and social assistance industries employ approximately 24 percent of Asbury's residents.[1]

The labor market in Asbury represents both the challenges and opportunities that the town exemplifies and the ways intersectionality frames the city and is amplified by the seasonality

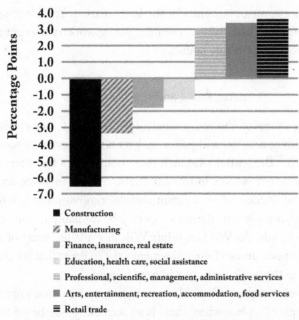

FIG. 13. Change in Asbury Park residents' industries of employment, 2008–2017. (Source: U.S. Census Bureau, 2008–2012; and *2013–2017 American Community Survey 5-Year Estimates*)

Note: Asbury Park residents sixteen years of age and older

of gentrification. In Asbury Park, the growing service base has struggled to provide real employment opportunities for the residents in town. However, this is not universally experienced, and there are groups of inhabitants—particularly those who are younger—who are able to gain some access to the local service jobs. In this chapter, we will hear from several West Side residents as they struggle to make ends meet in Asbury Park. They share their perceptions of and experiences with employment in the city, along with their hopes for their futures. We will examine how the experiences of workers and those of working age differ depending on a variety of circumstances. Here a lens of intersectionality highlights the nuanced impacts that seasonal gentrification processes can have on local residents. In what follows, we explore how certain residents—particularly younger people of color who can provide the aesthetic labor to the retail stores and bars—can experience some opportunity in the labor market. Yet this opportunity often excludes others; even the young workers who get the jobs are often seasonally bound.

Spatial, Racial, and Age Mismatch

Framing many of the larger discussions around urban employment among scholars and policy makers is the concept of spatial mismatch.[2] The spatial mismatch hypothesis argues that there are "fewer jobs per worker in or near Black areas than white areas" because of residential segregation and discrimination in housing markets.[3] Simply put, there are fewer jobs available in minority neighborhoods. As William Julius Wilson explains, many of the existing opportunities for employment exist in areas that are inaccessible to those who are most in need of work.[4]

However, Asbury Park, like other gentrifying cities, provides an example of a place where there is an increasing number of local businesses due to the city's redevelopment, and these jobs are all located within approximately one square mile. Several researchers have found that there tends to be an increase in retail services as businesses emerge to meet a rising service customer base.[5] This growth would then imply that there would be a comparable growth in local jobs. And many of these occupations typically have low entry-level requirements—making them, at least in theory, available to a wide variety of residents. Yet our research finds that adult Black West Side residents are underrepresented in many of the growing East Side jobs. Although the jobs are located in just over one square mile, this small geographic distance is often belied by the perceived (and often actualized) cultural and racial divides and disparities that are physically marked in space by the train tracks. As noted throughout this book, the train tracks in Asbury Park demarcate the East and West Sides in ways that enforce racial segregation. In many ways that we will explore, for West Side residents, it does not matter that the East Side jobs are just a short walk from West Side housing; the train track border exaggerates the distance in powerful ways.

As such, what is occurring in Asbury is more than just a spatial mismatch. We also frame the experiences of city residents within the context of a racial mismatch. As Hellerstein, Neumark, and McInerney explain, "The racial mismatch hypothesis suggests that the problem is not a lack of jobs, per se, where blacks live, but a lack of jobs into which blacks are hired, whether because of discrimination, labor market networks, or neighborhood effects in which race matters. Under the racial mismatch hypothesis, it is the local availability of jobs for (or held by) members of one's own race that matters for employment."[6] Yet in trying to access the opportunities in Asbury Park along the beachfront just across the train tracks, many Black residents face structural factors embedded within racial hierarchies and inequalities.

Moreover, as we will highlight throughout this chapter, the racial mismatch is further complicated by *the intersection* of age stratification. While the restaurant, beachfront, and boardwalk employees are often White middle-class young adults, we observe workers of color throughout the East Side hosting customers as they enter restaurants, working the splash pad, checking beach badges, acting as bouncers, and making lemonade at beachfront food stands. Overall, these workers of color, while local, are young—in high school and their early twenties. Age intersects with race to form an additional employment barrier for many long-time West Side residents while perhaps providing some opportunities for others.

Aesthetic Labor and Gentrification

The high-end boutiques, hotels, and cosmopolitan cocktail bars on Ocean Avenue and Cookman Avenue, the main tourist thoroughfares in Asbury, provide many jobs for the community. Like similar higher-end labor markets throughout the country, the workers are part of the brand that is being sold to customers—adding to the level of inequality in the labor market itself.

Indeed, tied directly to racial and age mismatch is the fact that the jobs available in Asbury are concentrated in the high-end service economy. Expensive restaurants, trendy hotels, posh boutiques, and chic coffeehouses dot the boardwalk and streets on the beachfront side. Many of these are small businesses that are central to the "charm" of the city. Asbury is charming a specific type of tourist and new resident, like the East Village and Wicker Park before it; the city is looking to attract a hip and edgy crowd.[7] As Arlene Davila has exposed regarding the Latinization of East Harlem, gentrifying communities often gentrify on the back of the very local culture that they then displace.[8]

The many recent articles inviting tourists to come to the "coolest" city or this "hipster" town demonstrate that the restaurants, hotels, bars, music venues, and stores in Asbury are selling an experience in addition to their craft beers, funky donuts, and designer dresses. For instance, *Travel and Leisure* magazine noted, "If it's possible for a town to have a je ne sais quoi, Asbury Park could be the East Coast's top contender."[9] And the food scene has rave reviews from foodies from the *New York Times* to *Food and Wine* magazine to local bloggers. As such, the workers who staff the stores, pour the drinks, and serve the meals in the restaurants have become de facto aspects of the town's overall feel and experience. The worker, as part of Asbury's brand, is a central piece of the gentrification process. In her ethnography of coffeehouse workers, Yasemin Besen-Cassino highlights that the need to create an experience is upfront in the hiring process. She shares a job ad that reads, "If you are looking for a fun place to work and be part of a team, we offer a great work environment."[10] Ironically, pay and skills are not part of the ad; instead, the *experience* of the work is paramount. As employers search for a "look" to apply to their stores and restaurants as opposed to skills and/or experience, White middle- and upper-middle-class young people have a distinct advantage over less affluent young people of color. Ben Cassleman finds that family income and race are important predictors of whether a young person has a summer job. Data from the Current Population Survey demonstrate that teenagers whose families make less than $20,000 per year are less than half as likely to work as those from families who earn at least $100,000. And Black and Hispanic teens have far lower employment rates than Whites.

Despite economically needing to work, these teens are often disproportionally underrepresented in the youth labor force.[11]

Asbury workers, like so many service workers, are often expected to look and act a certain way—referred to as aesthetic labor. Like in many low-wage jobs where one sells a "service," Dennis Nickson and his colleagues determine that the skills employers demand are social and aesthetic. Analyzing survey data from retail stores, hotels, bars, restaurants, and cafés in Glasgow, they find overwhelmingly that both interpersonal communication and self-presentation are central to service work. Close to all surveyed employers feel that social, interpersonal, and self-presentation skills are important. Conversely, slightly less than half of employers report that technical skills are important.[12] Indeed, the right appearance and personality take precedence over technical qualifications. Lynne Pettinger finds that sales assistants are a critical part of the "branding" of retail stores and that their social and aesthetic skills are central to their work. She concludes that "fashion orientation is one facet of brand-strategy [used by the stores] and the ability to present a fashionable appearance is one of the skills needed by sales assistants in many stores."[13] In Asbury Park, among the barriers many West Side residents may face in securing East Side jobs is that they do not fit the "brand" of Asbury that is being marketed.

As we show in this chapter, race matters, and race intersects with age in interesting ways in Asbury. In some ways, younger people of color appear to have an easier time securing jobs on the beachfront and in training programs. In contrast, older people of color—who ostensibly struggle to display the young, hipster brand of the town—often find themselves excluded from the work. In our conversations with West Side residents—predominately long-time Black residents—we attempted to understand their experiences in trying to secure work on the East Side and the way spatial and racial and age mismatch, along with the demands for aesthetic labor, impacted their job opportunities.

Of course, the first hurdle to employment is that one must have access to jobs. Many Black residents reported significant challenges in finding work on the East Side. This is striking considering the city's early economic development history, which was predicated on the cheap service-sector labor provided by Blacks from the West Side. However, as seasonal gentrification has taken place in the 2000s, many longtime West Side residents report that they have felt largely excluded from labor opportunities. They told us they face several obstacles to employment in the beachfront town, ranging from subtle microinequities to larger structural barriers, along with increased competition from White workers.

RACISM

Racial microinequities are significant factors that too often create an atmosphere in which people of color feel they do not belong. Of course, the microinequtities and racist aggressions that make individuals feel they are unwelcome are not unique to Asbury Park. In recent years, several examples have garnered national attention as White customers and managers have been caught on camera and outed on social media engaging in racist behaviors toward Black men and women as they attempt to live their daily lives—be it waiting at a Starbucks coffeehouse or picnicking in a public park. This has garnered much social media outcry, with videos of White people telling Black individuals to leave restaurants or other public spaces going viral. Hashtags such as #eatingwhileblack or #coffeewhileblack have been created for Black individuals to share their experiences of the challenges they face performing everyday activities. This racism is particularly acute in gentrifying communities, where White residents have called the police on Black people unnecessarily (#BBQBecky) and people of color have faced violence and even death.[14] The racialization of spaces—determining who belongs and who does not—is prevalent in public places throughout the United States and pronounced in gentrifying communities.

When we asked West Siders, particularly older residents, if they had ever worked on the East Side, we found resistance to the very idea of finding employment there based on perceptions of racism. One man reports, "It's too much racist . . . if you go down there. You're not dressed right. You don't look right." In fact, implicit bias extends far beyond West Siders' employment experiences to include their opportunities for leisure time in the many shops and restaurants. One resident shared that not only could she not get hired to serve food and drinks at the posh establishments; she was not served when she went inside as a customer:

> Horrible service. I went in [a restaurant] once . . . it was with two other people. . . . We went in, sat down, made a drink order, and didn't get our drinks. We were too busy talking, so we weren't really paying attention to the time. Other people came and sat [in the restaurant]. Next thing we know, they have food . . . I'm like, "What time did we come in here? Let's see what time we paid our parking," and it was a good forty minutes. . . . So we're like, "OK, let's go." And we just left.

The racial mechanisms that guide whether one can be served a drink at a restaurant while Black are magnified in the hiring process, and the end results are significant. One instrument of exclusion is the gatekeeping of hiring managers in the businesses on the boardwalk and downtown areas. A common pattern we encountered was that despite the business posting "Help Wanted" signs at the store and online, when West Side residents inquired about opportunities, they were often told that hiring was actually not happening. For instance, one resident notes, "I've gone in and, like, [the manager has said,] 'Oh, we're accepting applications, but we're not hiring right now,' and there'd be a nice little 'Hiring' sign in the window." Another recounts, "I've gone to, like, pick up an application for someone and, like, [the manager has said,] 'Oh, we can give it to you. We're accepting, but we're not hiring right now.' Meanwhile on Craigslist, there's just an ad put up less than five hours ago. I'm like, 'Oh, OK.'" This resident goes on to reflect, "So not only are you rude if I come here to eat, but you're also rude if I come here to apply for a job." Residents also describe feeling stereotyped: "First thing they say is we lazy. We don't want to work. If you're late, [they say,] 'Oh, he don't want to work.'"

One resident shares that he thought his background could be an asset to a boutique store in Asbury Park, but the owner did not see this value:

> When they opened, I was going to see if they were hiring because my thing is that you want to have all types of people working in your place because you want everyone to come there to feel comfortable coming there, and you want people to spend their money no matter who they are. Money is green. It doesn't matter who's giving it to you. But they were just like, "Oh, we're not hiring. All positions are filled." And there's like ten customers in the store and [there's] like one person and it's a small store, so it's like, "Oh, you guys don't need help? OK, that's fine."

Of course, the West Side residents' experiences also reflect larger racial discrimination in hiring. A 2017 meta-analysis of field experiments of hiring discrimination (individual résumé audits and in-person audits) found that Black and Latino discrimination has remained a significant structural barrier, with minimal improvement since 1989.[15] This indicates the endemic nature of racial discrimination in both our nation and the microcosm of Asbury Park.

CRIMINAL RECORDS

Another significant barrier to employment on the East Side occurs when applicants have a criminal record. Much research has demonstrated that criminal records serve as an impediment to employment throughout the nation. A 2017 Urban Institute report authored by Marina Duane notes how "criminal convictions have after-effects that extend far beyond the direct punishment imposed in the courtroom. These effects, commonly known as collateral consequences, disproportionately affect people who are low income and Black or Hispanic, who are also more likely to come into contact with the justice system."[16] According to a recent Center for American Progress (CAP) report, African American adults are five times more likely to be imprisoned than White Americans in the United States.[17] CAP's own research finds that African Americans are twice as likely as their White counterparts to have a family member imprisoned at some point during their childhood, along with overall incarceration rates that are more than 500 percent higher than they were forty years ago. CAP researchers conclude that Black millennials and postmillennials are at greater risk of contact with the criminal justice system than any previous generation. Our focus groups with West Siders highlighted not only the reality of mass incarceration in the Black community but also the collateral damage: many residents reported not being able to find or keep a job because of criminal records, even when those charges were decades old. This issue came up repeatedly and was clearly a difficult one for residents.

This is yet another example of how seasonal gentrification poses problems for local community members. The growing hospitality sector in Asbury Park does not appear to be one that welcomes hiring employees with criminal records. One challenge many residents face is that under the New Jersey Alcoholic Beverage Control (ABC) law, anyone who has been convicted or found guilty of a crime of moral turpitude, either in New Jersey or in another state, is disqualified from owning or being employed by a liquor-licensed business.[18] However, there is no clear definition of a "crime of moral turpitude"—it is a catchall. According to Andres Mejer Law, "A crime can qualify regardless of level of seriousness of the charge, or the sentence imposed for it, or the circumstances surrounding the commission of the crime."[19] The fuzzy legal definition makes it a somewhat subjective determination that can often be used to the determent of the worker.

For West Side residents of color already facing racism, criminal records create a barrier that feels impassable. A few workers discuss these dynamics in the focus group:

PARTICIPANT 1: Then you still roll and you still put in applications, and this goes for a lot of us in here, if your background . . .

PARTICIPANT 2: You know what I'm saying? I can't even mention that. With your background, you probably sold drugs.

PARTICIPANT 1: And by selling drugs to support our family, or we was addicts or using, it doesn't matter . . .

PARTICIPANT 2: . . . You go to jail, that background hurts you.

PARTICIPANT 1: Oh, yes, they hold it against you—even if it was thirty, forty years ago.

PARTICIPANT 2: You did the time.

This exchange highlights several important dynamics. Having a record—either recent or in the distant past—is a stigma that is difficult to break from. West Side residents who may have had convictions decades earlier report that they experience the same barriers as people with more recent sentences. The residents also highlight that even though they "did the time" and accepted responsibility, that was not enough. As the following exchange notes, the effects of their criminal records reverberate throughout their lives:

PARTICIPANT 1: So therefore, we be looking for a chance to renew [our lives] and start over.

PARTICIPANT 2: It's hard because they're not giving you that certain chance.

PARTICIPANT 1: They sure don't.

Some residents shared stories about the moment their employer found out about their criminal record. At times when they are fortunate enough to secure a job, or job offer, on the East Side, it could be rescinded. As these residents share,

PARTICIPANT 1: It's like they opened up that place over here off of Fifth Avenue and Kingsley. You know a lot of us was supposed to be the ones working. They said it's for Asbury.

PARTICIPANT 2: They called me up to say I was going to do the bussing, the cleaning, and everything, and they say, "Well, I see you got mechanic skills. We want an interview." I went for the interview. As soon as he found out about my background, I was right out the door.

Another woman describes how she got a job but was then fired when her background check came through: "I had got a job. I got in trouble twenty-three years ago, but now I started working. . . . Yeah, I made some mistakes. I had been good [working at the job] for about a month, and they found about my background, and they fired me." This case is particularly striking. Often the prospective employee is cautious about sharing his or her records from decades earlier. In this example, despite the fact that the woman's conviction was over twenty years ago and she had maintained a clean record since, her contributions to her current position were not enough to keep her job.

There are strategies that workers with criminal records can use to mitigate the impact of their record on employment. The U.S. Department of Labor's Federal Bonding Program offers fidelity bonds to employers to cover workers and insures ex-offender employees for between $5,000 and $25,000 for a six-month period.[20] This offers a route to employment for workers who would be considered "high risk" due to their criminal convictions. As residents explain,

PARTICIPANT 1: See, once you get bonded—which you gotta go down to [the neighboring town of] Neptune—if you get bonded, then they will hire you because it's a tax write-off and it's security. If anything you do wrong, they got to pay them for us.
PARTICIPANT 2: If you steal anything, if you quit, whatever. They got to pay them.
PARTICIPANT 1: That's insurance on that bond for them, not for you—for them.

When our conversation turned to bonding in the focus group, several participants were unaware of this possible route to employment. The discussion turned into an impromptu teaching session, with the residents with information on bonding sharing the process with the others. This exchange highlighted a key point: many residents are woefully unaware of programs that can mitigate some of the barriers they face. As one participant laments, "You know, a lot of people don't even know this [the bonding process]. Because of we being locked up . . . we don't know where to go and find it."

Indeed, education and awareness about ways to address the challenges workers with a criminal record experience are critical to reducing structural inequities. In addition to bonding, Asbury community groups, churches, and city officials offer several expungement workshops, providing opportunities for residents to learn about the expungement application process and meet with pro bono lawyers about their situation.

The obstacles these residents face are troubling, as much research has demonstrated that employment after incarceration is a key factor in reducing recidivism.[21] Employment helps stabilize individuals' lives, providing much-needed income, support, and a sense of community. Running criminal background checks and denying residents jobs—particularly based on offenses from decades earlier—continues to disadvantage certain groups as they attempt to rebuild their lives after serving their time.

Racial Discrimination in Jobs

Even West Side residents who do make it through the hiring hurdles still report racial inequities on the job. Our conversations with West Siders along with our own observations highlight how occupational segregation plays a significant role in employment opportunities. Residents who do find jobs often find themselves segregated into low-wage (often back-of-the-house) service work. One resident tells us, "Everything they want us to do—and I'm speaking from experience of color—is wash dishes and do housekeeping without moving up no ladder." This segregation is particularly evident in our focus group of Latina women, many of whom report that they work as housekeepers in hotels or wealthy private residences.

One woman shares how her working conditions are less than ideal: "For two months, I was working for one woman. She wouldn't give me a glass of water. She wouldn't give me a sandwich. She said, 'I'm going to pay you $15 an hour' and ended up saying, 'I'm paying you only $12 an hour.' Never offered me a glass of water."

The segregation of people of color—particularly women—in service work is not new. Sociologist Evelyn Nakano Glenn's classic work finds that White women tend to be in service jobs that are public facing, while women of color are overrepresented in "dirty back room" jobs, such as housekeeping and kitchen work.[22] More recently, in her ethnographic account of luxury hotel work, sociologist Rachel Sherman finds similar patterns today. She notes that hotel work is divided into two main categories: interactive and noninteractive. Interactive, or front-of-the-house, work consists mainly of intangible emotional labor, while back-of-the-house, noninteractive work mainly involves physical labor. Sherman shows that interactive workers are usually White (except for bellmen and door attendants, who provide more physical work and are usually men of color), and noninteractive workers are typically people of color and immigrants. In addition, Sherman notes the wage differences between these categories. Not only are back-of-the-house workers paid less than front-of-the-house workers (about one to two dollars less per hour); they also do not typically receive the tips that front-of-the-house workers obtain from hotel guests.[23]

Young, Hip Workers on the West Side

The workers highlighted thus far in this chapter were often older longtime residents of color. In many ways, their employment challenges are similar to workers outside of Asbury who have less formal education and criminal records and face age discrimination. There is significant literature on the ways age impacts access to jobs. Finding a job as one ages can be very difficult. Maria Heidkamp and her colleagues at Rutgers University's John J. Heldrich Center found that older workers who are unemployed are less likely to find new employment than younger workers who are unemployed.[24] Many older workers involuntarily work part time because they cannot find full-time employment. Others become discouraged and drop out of the labor force, believing that they will not find new jobs. Through surveys and interviews of older workers, Heidkamp finds that many of them believe age discrimination contributes to their failure to find a job. The question then intrigued us: Do younger workers from the West Side who are not well represented in our focus groups secure jobs more easily on the East Side?

From our observations, we could see how race and age intersect in the beachfront service jobs. While our waiters and waitresses and most salespeople were White, at a boutique hotel, we saw young, hip-looking men and women of color registering guests, and at the boardwalk restaurants, we saw similar workers greeting customers at the door and preparing food at beachfront food stands. These workers were in the front of the house in customer-facing jobs and were very much part of the experience that was being sold. We found that they often presented themselves in ways that were very congruent to Asbury Park's notion of "coolness." For example, they might be tattooed, pierced, wearing dreadlocks, or gender nonconforming. We also saw local Asbury students of color working at the splash park and checking badges on the boardwalk. Three young workers we spoke with proudly told us that they got their jobs through programs at their high school. Moreover, Asbury councilwoman Yvonne Clayton seemingly agreed with this assessment. She told us that over the summer of 2018, she had observed more local youth from Asbury working in jobs on the East Side and along the waterfront.

In many ways, these findings illustrate opportunity. Local Asbury youth of color can secure and maintain coveted summer jobs on the Asbury Park Boardwalk and beaches. We did not see or hear of any use of J-1 Visas, which are issued as part of educational and cultural exchange programs. Perhaps the public-private partnerships were bearing fruit, perhaps the training programs (discussed in chapter 4 in detail) were effective in placing local young people in jobs, perhaps these workers' connections with their schools help them navigate the barrier of the railroad tracks and the mismatch we observed with other workers, perhaps young people are demonstrating their value as employees, or perhaps the low unemployment rate in 2018 compressed the available labor pool. While all these factors could (and probably do) play a role in the increased representation of Asbury youth in local jobs, there seems to be something additional at play—namely, the intersection of youth, race, and coolness in Asbury.

Yasemin Besen-Cassino's work on youth and employment highlights the branding of young workers in the service economy. In her study of more affluent, predominately White young people, she finds that these employees choose to work in the service sector in part because they want to be associated with the employer's brand—whether it was a coffee company or a fashion designer. And from the employer perspective, the young workers become the ideal face of the products they are selling. Besen-Cassino notes that the distribution of these jobs to young people is very much race and class based. The retailers in her study, in trying to woo affluent White shoppers, find that hiring young workers who mirror that demographic can be appealing to those shoppers.[25] And certainly, many companies have faced legal action as a result of such discrimination. For instance, Abercrombie & Fitch, a clothing chain, has faced a number of lawsuits over discriminatory hiring practices. They have been accused of refusing to hire people of color for sales positions and in 2005 agreed to a settlement that included monetary damages as well as revising their hiring policies.[26] Not surprisingly, hiring practices often lead to a youth labor market where White and affluent workers are more likely to have summer jobs than their lower-income and/or Black and Brown peers.

While White hipsters and middle-class students held many of the jobs along the beach and boardwalk, we found that young local students of color were also visible in these jobs. In many ways, the hipster-cool brand of Asbury—particularly a town that is advertising acceptance and diversity as part of its brand—works to the advantage of local youth. In some ways, these workers can leverage their racial and sexual identities within the context of coolness. This commodification of diversity is part of the business plan, economic development, and workforce development of the city. The young workers from Asbury are able to fit the brand (i.e., trendy, edgy, diverse, tolerant, LGBTQ) of gentrification that is occurring. Expanding Besen-Cassino's argument makes clear that young workers of color may not be excluded from jobs—provided they can do the aesthetic labor of coolness. And that in itself can be challenging; they have to walk a fine racial line. "It's not a matter of whether you're black or not black. It's what kind of black person you are," Ted Thornhill, author of the study "We Want Black Students, Just Not You: How White Admissions Counselors Screen Black Prospective Students" tells the *Boston Globe*. "You have to be Condi Rice, not Angela Davis." Thornhill concludes, "In other words, be black—but not too black."[27] As evidence of this theory, young local workers in Asbury are able to secure jobs and navigate the White space because they are able to present their intersectional identities in ways that are not only congruent with the Asbury "coolness" but also acceptable to the predominately White patrons. They are able to do the aesthetic labor of coolness: their race along with their self-presentation with cool clothing, jewelry, and hairstyles and even gender fluidity contribute to the feeling of comfort with diversity that Asbury wants to project.

The importance of doing the aesthetic labor is most evident when we compare the young workers' experiences to those of the residents on the West Side. As noted, many of the older West Siders face multiple employment barriers: they are older, have criminal records, and would likely not be perceived as subjectively "cool" based on the East Side, middle-class, hipster standards. Years of living in poverty often make it difficult for these residents to mask the related challenges and obstacles. Long-term West Siders sometimes bear the racial history of the town on their bodies. As Chris Warhurst and Dennis Nickson note, aesthetic labor is about the style an employer is looking to sell.[28] Indeed, as Pierre Bourdieu writes, social class (among other things) is manifested through aesthetics, providing visual cues about one's social standing.[29] As such, poverty is often embodied. For example, a lack of access to health care contributes to health issues and physical scars of poverty, such as poor teeth.[30] Such indicators are impossible to cover up or "mask for the task."[31] In addition, culturally valued assets such as communication style and language may differ from socially privileged White middle-class norms.[32] So for the older workers, the signs of poverty and educational barriers they bear would likely not be considered cool or hip—and they are not aspects that middle-class, often White patrons want to be reminded of as they drink cocktails on the beach or shop for expensive sunglasses.

A tourist might enjoy having a waitress who is a local Asbury youth with trendy clothing and tattoos. Perhaps said tourist may even offer unsolicited advice about college choices or career options. There is a feeling of hope for this young employee that older adults in our focus groups might not elicit. A conversation with these older residents might force the tourist to acknowledge how decades of racism, inequitable educational opportunities, mass incarceration, and vast income disparities have shaped that worker's opportunities throughout his or her life . . . and that may be just too hard to swallow with a medium-rare tomahawk ribeye steak in one of Asbury's swanky restaurants.

Working Elsewhere

As a result of the lack of access to East Side jobs, some residents try to find whatever work they can on the West Side, where job opportunities are less than plentiful. As one resident illustrates, "So we have to eat, so what we do is we fall back to the West Side. . . . And we say to ourselves, 'We're going to come over here where I can go get some pizza and I can deliver' or 'I can go over here and make something under the table.' You know what I'm saying? Anything per diem to see we can take care of ourselves."

West Side residents often dream of and at times rely on the jobs that have historically been seen as the best employment options in the area, such as working in the local school system, holding local government jobs, or doing hospital work just outside of Asbury Park. Often, however, workers who attain these positions possess a set of skills or networks that set them apart from their peers. As one African American woman shares, "I worked with the [city] office on Bond Street, and they helped Asbury residents get jobs within the city. Public works needed someone that was good with computers, but they didn't have anyone except for me. So they kind of loaned me to public works, and then public works was like, 'You're not getting her back.' So I stayed there until money ran out from the housing authority."

After her job was defunded at public works, Hurricane Sandy hit the Jersey Shore, and additional grant money came into the city and nonprofits to assist in the recovery. She was then able to parlay her computer skills into a job with a community-based organization in the city. After that funding ran out, she learned of a job at the senior citizen center. While she does have a job, it is part time, and she does not have benefits or paid time off. So although she has income, she is not economically secure. Yet in many ways, she would be considered a "success" of public workforce development programs (i.e., education and job training programs) that focus on an immediate attachment to the labor market. What is further troubling is that public sector jobs, which were once the route to the middle class for many Black Americans are not the secure route they once were.[33] However, as noted earlier in this chapter, this is the largest industry of employment for residents in Asbury, with almost a quarter working in education, health care, and social assistance.

For many locals, despite the economic development in their community, they must look for employment outside of Asbury Park and face the major obstacle of transportation. Dependable transportation is something many residents do not have access to. Buses are not reliable for accessing these jobs, and so if one does not own a car, the options are limited. As one worker in a focus group explains about a recent demolition job, "All right, it was in Matawan [neighboring town]. So we started working, but from Matawan we had to go to Sayreville. So we was working, last week my car broke down, and I called them and told them my car broke down. That same night, he called me back and said, 'We can't use you no more'—and that job he was paying, we was making good money."

Other participants worked at a Walmart out of town and shared the challenges of irregular bus schedules. They were forced to spend a large percentage of their minimum-wage pay on a cab. One of them notes, "Uber drivers was taking all my money, so I had to quit." Another explains, "I moved down here probably about a year ago. It's not a lot of transportation down here. Everything runs like an hour. I'm used to buses running everything fifteen minutes. No . . . a lot of places buses don't go—like I had a good job, but I couldn't get to Holmdel [a neighboring town] every day."

Thus many companies offering entry-level jobs that are more likely to hire older workers—such as Walmart, large grocery stores, or fast-food chains—are not available to residents in Asbury Park. Walmart is not opening a superstore on the beachfront, and McDonald's (while there is one on the west side of town) is not going to serve its burgers alfresco next to the convention hall. In addition, there is no large supermarket in Asbury. To obtain employment, older West Siders need reliable transportation, which is not plentiful.

"I Gotta Eat; I Gotta Feed My Family"

As we spent time with the West Side residents, they shared how they perceived and processed the local Asbury labor market. Some of the residents we spoke with perceive racism as a significant barrier to jobs. As one West Sider sums up, "Like us, me . . . I'm good. I know how to do everything, but the eyes on us—like, we don't know how to do—and we can build everything, but they look at us like we're not fit for it, but we are capable of doing it. We was born with the roots." Another notes how he had to overcome racial stereotypes to be hired as a mechanic:

Now they said to me, "What can you do?" I said, "I can repair everything from a Ford Model T to a Jaguar. I have my own tools." They said, "Well, how can we be sure you know what you're doing?" Now this is what I had to do. I had to work for three days with no pay doing jobs on their cars to get the job, and that's not the first time I've had to. . . . But see, who's gonna complain? I gotta eat; I gotta feed my family. I have a car, but my car doesn't run on love, you know what I mean? It doesn't. I mean, I have grandchildren.

The residents are well aware of the racial history of Asbury and of their own challenges within the system. One resident notes the similarities between the exclusion from East Side opportunities today and those job opportunities that were part of the founding of Asbury: "But they said it was like that back in the day before, though. They kept all of us over here, and you couldn't even go across the tracks. I heard that you couldn't do anything, so that['s] coming back definitely because they're doing everything across the tracks, everything."

The racist history further amplifies the views the residents held on the gentrification they were experiencing. As the West Siders make sense of the impacts of gentrification, some note that the promises they heard from politicians about jobs in the local community actually translated into jobs for the gentrifiers. One woman tells us, "So now the White community has moved in, and they're buying up left and right. So now they're [people in power are] saying, 'Well, we're going to give jobs to people in the community'— [but it's] your White community. That's who you're giving your jobs to because that's a lot of what they're hiring in the Asbury Hotel is your White community."

Longtime residents also see the lack of jobs as related to the growing number of Latinos in Asbury Park—a racial tension that is evident in the town. As one resident says, "Us American people here, we're losing our jobs to all the illegals. That's not fair for us. See, they work for nothing, and they're willing to work all day and do whatever is necessary regardless, and lord knows, I'm not here to debate if they got their credentials or not. That does not matter. The bottom line is they can do the job, and they're willing to do the job." However, another Black resident challenges this statement: "A lot of us think that they [Latinos] can work for nothing, and I work with a few Mexicans. They get paid. We think they don't get paid, but they actually get paid. The thing is, they're considered a better worker than a Black person. They're considered more reliable."

One resident feels that resources such as small business grants can help move residents to the middle class: "The SBA, the small business administration, OK, now if you have—if you're an African American and you have been to prison, they consider you a level minority, OK, but I say I want to start a business right there. They won't give me it, yet Mexicans and others, they come over here, and they get everything." Despite the fact that there is very little evidence that Latino immigrants are displacing Black workers from jobs, the sentiment was palpable in Asbury Park. And while we were conducting our focus groups, the myths of immigrant invasions and Latinos taking jobs were fueled by Donald Trump, who was repeating and amplifying these claims to Black audiences.[34]

However, not all residents understand their experiences in this frame. Other residents see the issue as more than just Mexican residents taking jobs from longtime Black residents. One resident argues that the lack of education and experience impede many residents in her community. This focus group exchange highlights this sentiment:

PARTICIPANT 1: I kind of heard a little something yesterday. They were—I think one person was kind of blaming the Mexicans for taking all the jobs . . .

PARTICIPANT 2: You can't blame them because before they came, y'all had jobs. You ain't one of them, so don't get mad 'cause they got them.

PARTICIPANT 1: Exactly, and that's why I wanted to say that, but I said, "I'd probably start a whole riot out there."

FACILITATOR: Do you think that those are jobs that . . . people who aren't Latino or Mexican would take?

PARTICIPANT 1: They low-paying jobs. Me myself, I don't care if it's low in pay and it's a job. You gotta keep struggling in this world.

PARTICIPANT 2: They [longtime West Side residents] choose not to take it, and now the Mexicans [are taking the jobs, and so people say], "Oh, these people coming here taking our jobs." And then you want to go in if you think you're supposed to get a full-time job at $15 an hour and you have no education and you have no experience—that's just not the way it works. I think what needs to, and like we need to—some people need to be retaught how this thing works, and it doesn't work the way they want it to work.

What this exchange also demonstrates is a theme that emerged throughout our research: West Side residents rarely reported that systemic impediments to opportunity were the reason employment was so bleak. Interestingly, few of the workers identified their employment challenges as related to a lack of good employment opportunities and large income inequality. In contrast, the residents felt there was an opportunity on the East Side, and they were simply not part of that opportunity. They felt marginalized and left out of the growth on the East Side and underserved by resources like public transportation that would allow them access to good jobs elsewhere. In many ways, some residents still held on to the idea of the American Dream and then blamed themselves (or others from different racial backgrounds) when they did not achieve it. The divisions and distrust in the community run deep on this topic. One resident tells us that he is "not putting too much stock" in the promises that local residents would have access to jobs. As he aptly puts it, "Honestly, the promises—it wasn't for the West Side. The promises was for [the East Side]. So it doesn't matter to us. I mean, they wouldn't care what we say 'cause it's not for us. It's for them."

4

Owning a Business

The Employers' Side

While we found distinct patterns of intersectionality in the work opportunities and experiences of residents of Asbury Park, the economic development policies of the city are focused on uniting the city as one. In November 2017, city leaders commissioned a workforce development plan, strategically titled "One Asbury." According to the plan, the key policy goal of the city should be to eliminate the East and West Side segregation and unite Asbury Park as one community. By placing that policy goal directly within the workforce development system, the connection among residential segregation, racial segregation, and labor market segregation is identified as a problem. The authors of the plan assert that Asbury's segregation is a key factor impacting the economic well-being of the city. Taken to its logical conclusion, racial and income inequality are bad not just for residents but for economic development. Central to the workforce development system is a mandate to engage in public and private partnerships that directly support residents' access to skills training and Asbury Park jobs. Implicit in this recommendation is that the city needs to support businesses to increase opportunities for local labor. In many ways, the problem is framed as a skills gap issue: providing training opportunities will better prepare local workers for jobs. While there may be a skills gap, particularly customized skills for local businesses, we question whether that is the only gap and if public-private partnerships are a panacea.

It is against this backdrop that we met with local business representatives in the city. We spoke with owners and managers to better understand how they viewed local hiring and to get a sense of their experiences and their concerns. In this chapter, we share their perspectives. Over the course of our ethnographic exploration of the city, we predominately interviewed employers on the East Side. We share their challenges and successes in reaching out to, hiring, and working with local residents. Central to this chapter are two distinct yet related workforce programs, both of which are very much in line with the recommendations of the workforce development plan: the Salt School for the Asbury Hotel, Asbury Ocean Club, and Asbury Lanes—posh boutique hotels and a bowling alley on the East Side—and the Kula Café, a local establishment on the West Side. These two case studies illustrate the different ways that private-public partnerships are implemented on both sides of the tracks.

Gentrification and Business

Asbury Park's character is in part related to the eclectic restaurants, coffee shops, and boutiques that service the growing tourist base. Asbury prides itself on its collection of local businesses, the owners of which typically espouse liberal and progressive views. For instance, the Asbury Park Women's March after President Trump's election in 2016 was organized by four local women business owners who were frustrated with the election results. In addition, some small business owners were members of organizing committees for the rallies protesting ICE immigration policies in 2018. Others participate in environmental initiatives, help provide meals to the community, and spearhead arts programs and other initiatives to address larger systemic problems in Asbury and beyond. In fact, Marilyn Schlossbach, the owner of several restaurants in town, has published a cookbook, *Feed This Community: My Life in Food and Community with a Dash of Fun*, detailing her life in the food industry and the ways to "feed" that back to the local community through support.[1]

In our conversations with these progressive small business owners, while they reported a strong affinity to the town, they also faced significant challenges—many of them tied to seasonal gentrification. The popularity of Asbury has led to what some call an oversaturation of business: "There are now TOO many coffee shops and bakeries. Competition is usually good for everyone. But when TOO many coffee shops open, there just isn't enough business to go around."[2] Many of the business owners with whom we spoke lamented the parking challenges that impacted both their workers and customer base. And the low-priced rents that made Asbury affordable for entrepreneurs in 2011 were being replaced by much higher rates, forcing some businesses to close or relocate.[3] Across our discussions with business owners, activists, and residents, all noted that the majority of businesses along Ocean and Cookman Avenues were White owned. In terms of hiring, all the business owners stated that they wanted to hire locally. And some did. Yet many described the challenges they experienced hiring locally and the ways they processed those challenges. As one activist tells us, "It's mostly, like, progressive White folks or well-meaning White folks that are creating jobs for Black folks or low-income folks. And not as a critique, but that's kind of what's happening."

HOW SMALL BUSINESS OWNERS DEFINE GENTRIFICATION

To begin, it is important to explore the often complicated relationship between local businesses and the gentrification in town. All the business owners we met were, not surprisingly, aware of this phenomenon. Several of the owners tried to make sense of the process—which provides customer markets for their goods and services—in ways that acknowledged the economic benefits and privileges for their businesses, but they also recognized how gentrification is contributing to the growing inequity in a town they care about. For instance, one restaurant owner notes, "So I would say what's good about the development is . . . I mean, when we came down here ten years ago, this was all boarded up. So obviously, like, even talking about, like, gentrification and all of that, I would say there [were] no businesses. There were like, no residents down here, so the fact that these businesses were created and created jobs I think is great and . . . kind of the buzz that's around here."

Clearly, this small business owner believes that the seasonal gentrification over the past decade brought "buzz" to the town. In that way, they see gentrification as a positive force bringing in customers to the restaurant and other businesses in Asbury. However, this owner went on to note that with seasonal gentrification comes challenges, particularly segregation: "There is a huge divide in this town. It [is] literally the west side of the tracks out here, so I would say that it isn't a great feeling to see that . . . there's obviously some development in some areas and some not. So I think even just dealing with kind of the difficulties of that and figuring out a solution to how to kind of make a healthy development rather than just like a displacement [is needed]."

Indeed, many of our interviewees were aware of the segregation in town. In many cases, the business owners tried to frame themselves as welcoming and working to address the problem. This was perhaps most evident in our conversations with a shop owner who chose the geographic location of their business based on the city's bifurcation. This owner tried to straddle both sides of town, envisioning their shop as serving both the longtime residents and the newly arriving gentrifiers. They explain, "And so we consciously chose this area in Asbury because it's neither east nor west. It's actually in the heart [of the town], so our clients that felt disenfranchised and could not come downtown because they didn't feel very welcomed could easily cross the tracks and come here and talk about wellness. At the same time, our clients driving a Mercedes, BMWs, and stuff could come from these other outlying regions and not feel threatened by being here at the time." This owner feels that locating near Main Street was more than just a business decision to increase market share; it was a social justice choice too.

The shop produces and sells health foods, and the owner frames access to healthy foods as part of a food justice program.

While some business owners saw the positive aspect of gentrification, the growing income inequality accompanying the changes also posed serious challenges for them. Perhaps the growing inequality coexisting with business opportunities is best summed up by the following exchange:

FACILITATOR: So what's the best part of running a business here in Asbury?

PARTICIPANT: I mean, being part of the Asbury community. Asbury is just an incredible place to be. So it's where I've chosen to make my home and where I've chosen to start my business. . . . It's a very diverse community. It is not a cookie-cutter, suburban community, although we're probably technically a suburban area in Monmouth County—but it's a very urban environment that has aspects of city life, but you're half a mile from the ocean.

FACILITATOR: What is the biggest obstacle in running a business here in Asbury?

PARTICIPANT: It's the same answer. It's the same answer. It is a . . . very diverse community. You have . . . a lot of haves and you have a lot of have-nots. This particular street is a street that's struggling, I think.

FEAR OF BEING PUSHED OUT

Many of the small business owners we spoke to desired to ensure that development in town was "healthy." Some were genuinely conflicted about the gentrification that was occurring and its impact on residents and the culture of the town. Would the gentrification eventually push them out? One employer shares,

Sadly, I think that the two main areas right now are the boardwalk and the downtown, and I think that it's just gonna continue to expand, and I think that it's gonna become more expensive to live in certain areas. But I think that at the end of the day, it's going to be one of the top places to go on the Jersey Shore and to vacation. And there's going to be more people coming down from New York, and . . . I'm hoping that it's like—I think it will still be kind of like an interesting, weird place. . . . But I mean, in terms of gentrification, I feel like it will eventually be gentrified.

Small business owners feared that they could be forced to move because of rising rents. This concern is well founded in a gentrifying community, as much has been written about how small and local businesses close in favor of high-end chain stores in moderate-to high-income neighborhoods.[4] Many of the owners raised concerns about the beachfront development, with its million-dollar condos and high-end rents.

In some ways, the small business owners saw their work as not just running a business but contributing to the community. For instance, several owners of arts and music venues spoke of plans and initiatives to increase West Side residents' access to the arts—with mixed results. They reported that they would invite young residents into their establishments and show them how to paint, play an instrument, or develop another talent, and then after sharing the time, as one owner tells us, "It's literally like, 'OK,' and then I never see them again. So it is a [frustrating] thing because there's some people—they have super raw talent."

Some of these programs may have been unintentionally framed within a White gentrifier's context and not one that represented or had buy-in from the local community. For instance, one business owner framed her outreach to local residents as "I'm the type of person if I'm going to go on an adventure, I'm going on an adventure." She reported that she reached out to community groups and local churches yet did not have much success. With us, she reflects on the past racial divide but is not fully convinced that historical segregation should still be impacting residents today: "You know what I mean? Like I don't—I don't understand, like, 'Oh, I'm not allowed over there' or 'You're not allowed over here,' so it is challenging, and I do think that there are people who do like that racial divide. And I—you know, to me, it just doesn't make sense. It's like I understand historically why there's a divide here. . . ." Additionally, some employers say that the West Side residents simply may not want to take jobs on the East Side.

While several of the small business owners tried to walk the fine line between business and social justice interests, at least one blatantly questioned the idea of "well-meaning business owners." This owner shared a common critique of liberal policies that do not actually address economic opportunities or agency but instead take a more paternalistic approach: "You know, you have some local businesses that will say, 'Well, we're giving away Thanksgiving dinners,' or 'We're giving away Easter dinners,' or 'We're sleeping on the boardwalk to help the homeless,' but where are you hiring? You know, you may be helping the homeless, but are you developing the local talents? You know they're hiring international students to come in . . . and sending out requests for people to house them for [an] amazingly little amount of money, but you're sleeping on the boardwalk to help the homeless. I mean, you know."

This critique, not unique to Asbury Park, was evidenced in a variety of community programs in town. Robin DiAngelo's *White Fragility*, written directly to White liberal individuals, highlights this tension.[5] And while the term *White privilege* has increasingly entered the lexicon and even the 2019 Democratic Primary presidential debates, the challenges of acknowledging the ways White individuals—even those who believe they have the best of intentions—participate in racist systems remain significant and was at times quite evident.[6] As DiAngelo writes, "To the degree that white progressives think we have arrived, we will put our energy into making sure that others see us as having arrived."[7] This is in part contributing to the challenges business owners are facing in bringing more local residents into their establishments—both as patrons and as workers.

Asbury Hotel and Kula Café: Two Case Studies

The Asbury Park local government has collaborated with employers to develop workforce development plans to recruit and retain local labor. Two innovative programs that have accomplished success in this area are the Kula Café and the Salt School for the Asbury Hotel and Lanes (and, when it opened, the Ocean Club), albeit on different sides of the town and with different approaches. The Kula Café is located on the West Side, while the Asbury Hotel is situated just a block from the boardwalk on the East Side. The Kula Café, located on the ground floor of a public building housing senior and social service programs, has outdoor seating that looks out to the Springwood Avenue park (featured in chapter 2). Alongside the Kula Café is the Kula Urban Farm, a community garden growing fresh foods for the café and the city residents. In contrast, the Asbury Hotel is a hip, modern, boutique hotel complete with a rooftop bar, $400 a night rooms during the peak summer season, and modern artwork. There is an art store attached to the hotel that houses vintage rock 'n' roll pictures and albums of Bruce Springsteen and other Asbury bands, and on a busy Saturday night, one can see a mix of tourists walking around with mojitos, a bridal party or two, a wealthy family from northern New Jersey, and some local professionals hanging out in the lobby listening to acoustic guitar.

Yet both businesses, one nonprofit and one profit based, pride themselves on a community workforce development agenda. They both provide training to local residents for jobs in their businesses and in the broader hospitality sector in town. Although they have the same goal—employment opportunities for local residents—Kula and the Salt School have their fair share of differences, but in both cases, the obstacles they face speak to broader challenges in the city.

KULA CAFÉ

In April 2013, Interfaith Neighbors opened the Kula Café. Their mission is twofold. First, Kula provides a sixteen-week training program to prepare local youth, generally between the ages of eighteen and twenty-one, for available job opportunities in nearby restaurants in the shore communities as front-of-house workers— servers, bussers, and hosts. Kula is predicated on the idea that all too often, businesses will only look to hire those with experience, and it can be very hard to build experience if no one is willing to provide the opportunity. The café bridges that gap by providing a job-training program to prepare young people to enter the workforce in the hospitality trade. Interfaith also runs a business development center out of the facility, offering mentoring and office space to early-stage entrepreneurs. Second, Kula provides healthy food at an affordable price and aims to do so in a welcoming environment. Kula Café and the Springwood Center are an easy walk from the Asbury Park train station on New Jersey Transit's Coast Line.[8] There is hope that the community at large will come to embrace the mission of the café and recognize it as a "third place"—somewhere to relax and grab a coffee away from home or work.

Kula takes its mission seriously. In addition to selling food, Kula staff feed those who cannot afford the salads and sandwiches that for sale. Every Monday, soups, pastries, sandwiches, and juice are offered at no cost to those most in need. When available, Kula also distributes other goods accumulated through donations. In 2014, the *Asbury Park Press* teamed up with Interfaith Neighbors to help construct the Kula Urban Farm on Springwood Avenue. The Urban Farm provides not only fresh food and vegetables to residents and local restaurants but also training in growing organic food. The Kula staff utilize hydroponics and a vertical system to help maximize space.

Overall, Kula boasts of significant success. One of the leaders shares, "So we had about a hundred people come through the Kula Café program in five years, and if the youth complete the training program, 95 percent of them end the program with a job—full-time job." What leads to such an accomplishment? Our conversations with Kula Café developers highlight several important aspects of the partnership. First, the program is not only locally based; it is designed to address just job needs and the structural barriers that impact job success. As one of the leaders tells us, "There's a difference between the federal government–funded workforce development program and a workforce development program that has been developed to meet a specific local market need. Too many of the government-funded programs are training for training sake that don't lead to a job."

This is the heart of the job-training program. Not only does the Kula program tie training to local jobs in hospitality; the organizers are also careful to note that training is not enough. Instead, they provide wraparound services and referrals to help ensure that that the city residents can stay employed. As Walter "Chip" Clarke, associate executive director of Interfaith Neighbors, notes, a key to their success is having a youth specialist work with the students:

This is the heart of the job-training program. Not only does the Kula program tie training to local jobs in hospitality; the organizers are also careful to note that training is not enough. Instead, they provide wraparound services and referrals to help ensure that that the city residents can stay employed. As Walter "Chip" Clarke, associate executive director of Interfaith Neighbors, notes, a key to their success is having a youth specialist work with the students:

> We have a youth specialist here on staff who develops relationships with youth as they go through their training program. She's also the person that maintains contact with them—regular contact—after they've completed [the program] and got placement in [another] job. We maintain contact with them for no less than one year after their completion with us, and then the timeline of that contact starts as very intense. . . . We keep up with them on a monthly basis initially, and then [it] goes to every three months or so for the rest of that time just to check in. . . . It's part and parcel of the trust relationship, where you have to earn the trust of that young adult. You have to show them that

you care, and you can't just care for the sixteen weeks of the program. That trust factor goes far. . . . In one way, it's knowing that you're called [a] "youth specialist" twenty-four hours a day, seven days a week. . . . She continues to reach out to them after the fact and will call them and say, "Are you still working? What's going on? Are you having any problems?" And [she] really draws information out of them until they now revert to calling her when they have a problem instead of waiting for her to call them.

Another important factor in the Kula success, the advocates argue, is that the café is located on the West Side, recruits from the West Side, and conducts training on the West Side. Kula staff are part of the West Side community. Whereas East Side employers may be searching out a particular aesthetic labor that may not align with the West Side workers in need of employment, Kula staff reach residents where they are, a fact that is highlighted in the following exchange:

STAFFER 1: We've made this space available for that specific purpose. So I maintain that if there's a local business person that really wants to hire locally, they can find a way to do it.

STAFFER 2: That works well, by the way, because I think it does address these problems the residents perceive—they're not welcome, or so forth, and so on. They're really important here.

STAFFER 1: You've got to see the reality for what it is and then find the opportunity in the reality. So in an analogous situation, we had people in the arts community who said, "We want to expose the local youth—West Side youth—to the arts." They came to us out of frustration at one point and said, "We're really frustrated. We have this program. We have these classes. We hosted them on a gallery at the East Side." I said, "Stop right there. You're hosting it on the East Side. You need to come to the West Side."

STAFFER 2: The reality of the situation is if you want to make a local West Sider comfortable in your environment, you've got to reach out to them. You've got to bring yourself to where they are community first, establish the relationship, and then you may stand some success at getting them to come to the East Side.

By providing local youth with the training and jobs in the local community, Kula staff can address the work experience and skills that several employers have argued are lacking:

> Our youth come through, and they go through our sixteen-week program, where we introduce them to working in a functioning café. When they first begin, it's more observing than anything else. A big barrier that our youth typically encounter when they come in is being uncomfortable in a customer service role— having to talk to people that they're not familiar with—so we let them ease into that. Then we just work them through every position you would find in a restaurant. They learn to serve. They learn to clean. They learn to cook, prep, answer phones, [take] orders, all of that. But we kind of graduate them through it, so they see where it's comfortable. We will let them gravitate in a certain direction if that's where their strength seems to be, although we encourage them to do everything, front and back. But if they seem like they're really well suited for the back of the house, we'll allow them to spend the majority of their time in that area.

One nineteen-year-old West Side resident who previously held jobs at a warehouse, at a farm stand, and at Sky Zone (a trampoline park) notes the difference he experienced at Kula: "Other places, they just get straight to the point: Do your job. Here, I have to learn a lot about the restaurant business. And they taught me how to talk to people—how to deal with confrontation."[9]

While this program provides a promising model, it will not single-handedly solve the issues of inequity and unemployment in Asbury Park. Some focus group residents knew of the program but seemed wholly uninterested; others were unaware that the program existed. A small business owner expressed a disconnect between what she was hoping for in terms of fit (e.g., aesthetic labor) for a new employee and the potential employee that was sent from Kula, demonstrating the chasm that Kula graduates must still cross to attain employment. While the café is serving a much-needed purpose in the community, we certainly never saw it overflowing with customers, and we know that financing will always be at the forefront of planning for a local nonprofit like this one that does not garner the huge media attention and allure of the work development program we discuss in the following section.

SALT SCHOOL

While the Kula Café is located on the West Side, the Salt School trains workers for jobs at the posh Asbury Hotel, Asbury Ocean Club, and Asbury Lanes on the East Side. The Asbury Hotel's tall glass ceiling lets in the warm summer sun. There are pool tables, lots of books, a bar stocked with top-shelf liquors, and comfortable couches for guests to relax with a coffee or a locally crafted donut. The hotel also boasts a rooftop bar that is open during the peak summer season and gives guests a 360-degree view of the city. In one quick rotation, patrons can take in the beaches of the East Side and then look over toward the Kula Café and the West Side.

The Asbury Hotel opened Memorial Day weekend in 2016. With a commitment to hiring locally, the hotel took a unique approach. The Salt School was founded as a community initiative between the Asbury Hotel and the developer iStar to address the need for local labor. The free ten-week Salt School program was created as part of a workforce development plan to train area residents in the hospitality industry. The Salt School worked closely with the Boys & Girls Club of America and industry friends to prepare the training course. Organizers advertised widely and were featured in the *Asbury Park Press* and local TV news. The school enrolls applicants each spring in preparation for the summer season. As of this writing, there have been three Salt Schools with about three hundred graduates. In spring 2019's graduating class, there were eighty-nine graduates—80 percent of whom were slated to go on to work in the hotel, the bowling lanes, or the Ocean Club.[10] In subsequent years, the Salt School has not only continued its entry-level hospitality program but also developed a leadership program for some of its promising employees. The school is proud to welcome all types of individuals and encourages diversity.

Throughout our research, we observed that Salt School workers proudly display tattoos, dreadlocks, and jewelry that demonstrate their individuality; they also fit very much into the edgy, cool image of Asbury. In short, they are doing the aesthetic labor that fits with the Asbury Hotel and the style of the properties. Their very diversity, as noted in the previous chapter, is part of what is being sold. Again, this forced us to harken back to our conversations with the middle-aged Black West Side residents. A fifty-year-old mechanic with ongoing dental or medical issues may struggle to be hired to greet guests at the front desk of a posh hotel. A forty-five-year-old single mother struggling with childcare issues probably isn't going to be serving drinks at the rooftop bar. Thus opportunity cannot always be easily equally distributed in the training program—a fact that was roundly criticized in several of our focus groups and interviews.

While the Salt School (and Kula Café) are powerful examples of what can be done, there are bigger challenges that are endemic to our racially and socioeconomically stratified country that these programs alone will not fix. While providing space for community functions, holiday gifts to children in need, or fresh food to the community and training hospitality workers are incredibly worthwhile pursuits, these actions do not address the systems that fuel inequity. As one activist notes, "I think all the people that are doing really great work, the White progressive folks—it's needed, you know, but it also needs to talk of how we organize for systemic change for Black power to come."

Providing access to jobs is critical and can have long-term effects. However, while the Salt School trains locals, creates jobs, and serves as a good community partner, the powers behind it are also building multi-million-dollar properties that local employers and potential employees will likely never be able to afford. This development leads to an increased cost of living citywide. And when developers have decades-long tax abatements that lead to less public funding for schools and other local programs, the community suffers for generations.

Challenges to Local Hiring for Employers

While the Kula Café and the Salt School have developed workforce development plans to recruit, train, and hire local workers, several of the small business owners we met with in Asbury Park did not have the resources or even understanding to do so. For instance, one owner explains that while they wanted to "do the right thing," they were just trying to keep their businesses afloat and did not have the bandwidth to navigate the existing workforce programs: "I would say, like, even in the beginning, [there] are programs to train people from the West Side in hospitality. I'm the type of person where, like, obviously I see the problems in Asbury, and I want to be a part of helping it, but I think that then you open a business for the first year, and you're just so inundated—and so like, to kind of engage with those programs just seems like I'm trying to just open this business and figure stuff out."

A key point here is that this business owner, again like the others in this chapter, clearly states that they "see the problems in Asbury" and wants "to be part of helping it." However, other circumstances (e.g., the stresses of opening a new business) makes this impossible. Another new business owner echoes this concern:

> I would say even when you guys bring up these topics, I'm very aware of everything that's going on, and I'm also involved in a lot of the gentrification, and it's something that I think about. I think that when you open a business and you're stressed, you're more likely not to engage or try to make change, and you're more [likely] just to make decisions based on wanting to make a bottom line. I find myself not being as compassionate but being open to these things because I would love to maybe give—hire

someone from the West Side—but I'm just thinking of like my business.

Interestingly, both of these owners juxtapose the success of their businesses with the challenges of hiring local residents. In both cases, they define themselves as caring and compassionate but note that the reality of their own struggles leaves them no time to engage in the real work needed to address the hiring disparities. This echoes the frame that DiAngelo highlights in *White Fragility*. The owners feel they need to take care of their businesses first before taking on the "hard work" of hiring local labor. So perhaps it is better to hire someone without those challenges and find less intrusive ways (such as donating food or space) to ease the racial tensions that exist.

Of course, that is not to say that there are not significant challenges to operating a small business (particularly in a rapidly changing and seasonal community) and for an owner trying to hire local labor. Indeed, some owners who did want to hire local shared some of the challenges they faced. Several employers spoke about structural barriers—transportation and housing—that lead to unstable employment patterns. One particularly inventive employer who did identify that structural barriers were a significant obstacle for local workers decided to find a solution by providing housing, mirroring the kind of necessary wraparound services Kula provides. The owner states, "When they [employees] need housing—like we have some guys from Haiti, found out one was living in a car. I said, 'We have a carriage house. Take it for the winter.' A neighbor called the town, said, 'She's in violation of Airbnb [policies in Asbury].' But that's my home, I'm not renting it, and actually that young Black man is my guest."

This business owner tried to address the housing challenge herself by sharing her own housing with a worker. In this case, she clearly saw the connection between employment and stable housing and worked to remedy the situation and address a larger structural inequality. However, sharing one's space for free is not a sustainable plan for all small business owners. As she explains,

"Now my mission is to find a home in Asbury Park for my employees. [They] used to pay $600 a month for a room. [Another] pays something like $1,400 for a two room, for him and his mom. He's a high school student, by the way, and I'm like, 'Well, why don't we buy a house for our employees, create a nonprofit, and then their money that goes into it can actually go toward their American dreams so when they want to leave, they would get a percent back?'"

Certainly, the overwhelming majority of business owners cannot provide housing or provide legal services to expunge criminal records, and they cannot be expected to. However, these barriers are real, and the engagement of the owners with a racial literacy lens is critical. Engaging the residents and organizations already in these businesses to come up with systems-based solutions can be a first step in providing support to small business owners who want to hire locally but are strapped for resources to devote to this process.

Racial Coding of Skills

One of the more insidious ways that racism seeps into the hiring process concerns the perception of workers' skills. Several business owners report that a lack of work experience proved to be a potential barrier for locals. One restaurant owner tells us, "When I'm looking at their [an applicant's] résumé, I'm always thinking where they've bartended before, how many years of experience do they have, and I will take someone that has multiple—like more years of experience—over someone that wants to try it for the first time."

Of course, programs that involve training (such as the Salt School and Kula Café) are addressing this gap, customizing training to the business. However, in addition to the work experience gap, we hear the typical calls for "professional skills." Yet these skills are often hard to define and racially coded. Indeed, the *racialized* social construction of skills overlaps extensively with racial and ethnic discrimination. First, despite popular discourses of "postracialism" and "color-blindness," discriminatory attitudes continue to impact the labor market.[11] Job segregation and unequal outcomes occur even after controlling for other factors.[12] Employer hiring studies using matched résumés and/or "testers" (actors trained to play job applicants with identical qualifications) differing only in race or ethnicity are particularly instructive. In his 2007 paper, Marc Bendick summarizes the results of ten Black-White and six Anglo-Latino comparisons from the United States. Except for one study, the results uniformly show a White advantage, ranging from 2 to 38 percentage points (this "net rate of discrimination" is the difference between the percentage of employers who contacted the White/Anglo and the proportion who contacted the Black/Latino applicant).[13] Further research Bendick conducted with Rekha Eanni Rodriguez and Sarumathi Jayaraman continues to replicate and extend these findings.[14]

Nationally, employer interview research suggests that these employers, including those who are sympathetic to workers of color, often make a connection between a racial group's soft skills and their culture. In in-depth interviews, a substantial minority of U.S. and U.K. employers state assessments of the relative quality of workers from different racial groups.[15] Phillip Moss and Christ Tilly note that such studies find two kinds of employer perceptions of the skills of workers of color: skill hierarchy (which in the United States generally rates Whites and Asians highest, Latinos in between, and African Americans at the bottom) and skill fit (seeing particular groups of workers as well suited to particular kinds of jobs—for instance, viewing immigrant Latinos as ideal for difficult, low-paid manual work). Even where immigrant workers of color are seen as more motivated and therefore well suited to certain jobs, this skill stereotyping is associated with lower pay.[16] In the studies reviewed by Philip Moss and Chris Tilly, employers not only link soft skills to culture but often speak of cultural "fit" as a major hiring criterion.[17]

In addition, employers in several interview-based studies mention the growing importance of soft skills, particularly in entry-level and customer-facing jobs—in the same conversations in which many of them rate African American workers worse on soft skills.[18] For instance, Moss and Tilly and Rodger Waldinger and Michael Lichter show that managers in customer-contact jobs seek a racial-ethnic mix of employees with whom customers will feel comfortable; since Whites outnumber Latinos and Blacks and have greater purchasing power, this then privileges White individuals in these jobs.[19] These findings are also supported in a literature review conducted by Chris Warhurst, Chris Tilly, and Mary Gatta.[20] Summarizing existing studies by Harry Holzer and Michael Stoll, they find that a significant proportion of employers believe that customers, employees, or other employers prefer to deal with members of their own racial or ethnic group; that the probability of hiring a Black applicant for an entry-level job increases if the customer base is also Black; and that employers are less likely to hire Blacks and Latinos for entry-level jobs in suburban locations. Such findings have significant implications for the hiring of local Black residents on the gentrified East Side of Asbury Park.[21]

Moreover, job quality, workplace environment, and mode of supervision tend to elicit some specific types of worker responses. Employer observations of soft skills may be endogenous, creating environments that are ripe for the possibility of a self-fulfilling prophecy. For example, Elaine McCrate points out that if Black workers are monitored more closely for dishonesty, they are more likely to get caught, which then reinforces a stereotype of Black dishonesty.[22] More generally, Whites are observed serving the public in certain roles, which bolsters the perception that Whites are better suited to those roles.

Segregated and unequal processes even more strongly shape soft skill acquisition. Soft skills are in many cases an example of habitus that is molded by upbringing, peer culture, and early work experience.[23] To the extent that our society is segregated by race, those from minoritized backgrounds will typically be less fluent in the dominant White culture that sets norms and expectations in most employment settings. Workplace segregation can reinforce these processes: for example, giving White individuals' preferential access to customer-facing positions helps them develop abilities and secure greater opportunities. And as Chris Warhurst, Chris Tilly, and Mary Gatta note, in the new social construction of skills, workers of color are deemed less skilled than White workers and consequently experience discrimination.[24] The pervasiveness of such biases reinforces systemic racism in the labor market and workplaces.

This precariousness is evidenced by the Asbury employers. One owner explains what they termed "uncomfortableness": "I do think that on the West Side, there's like an uncomfortability of even them like, kind of engaging in this side. So it's like, you have to really seek out and like, engage in those programs and like, when I'm a business owner, I'm kind of like, I'm just trying to, like, get things off the ground." Another more directly shares what he or she feels is lacking in the local labor market:

> Cultural training is needed. We're not putting an ad on Craigslist saying we only hire White affluent people—we want people who are hungry and want the growth. With that in communities like Asbury Park and across the country there are . . . challenges. The work ethic in general is very different now than twenty years ago—technology has shifted that, instant gratification. While I'm a democrat, the welfare system has shifted that. I'm not a big proponent of giving things to people who don't deserve [them]. I've hired women in this community: "I don't need to listen to you because you are just a millionaire, and I can go and have another baby and get the check" . . . I want people to want to earn the check. I don't have a degree; I work seven days a week. There are others from this community who work so hard.

Indeed, the tension between systems of inequality and individual choice pervades the labor market. Business owners agree that housing, schools, and other institutions are problematic and that gentrification is negatively impacting residents on the West Side. However, when it comes down to it, many still see issues of criminal activity, reliance on public aid, and lack of education as individual choices. As another owner tells us, "[Community groups] were doing this hospitality training for people on the West Side, and I know, obviously, when the whole mentality there is crime, and there is drug dealing over there, and it gives kids access to make fast cash, which is what a lot of people do around here."

This owner points to the crime, applauds the training programs for young people, but in the end feels that the "fast cash" from drugs is too appealing to the young people. In many ways, the informal criminal economy can be a powerful draw and, some would argue, a logical choice—especially when one needs to put food on the table and does not have access to good-paying jobs in the formal economy. However, as long as engaging in what societal norms define as deviant behavior is framed as an individual choice, it is harder to see those structures of inequity.

This framing may also limit the effectiveness of workforce training programs that are designed to mitigate the problem. Employers step away from training because they understand that the acquisition of ascribed skills and cultural capital takes time and is so many ways racially coded. Employers still want these skills in their employees but would rather hire workers who already fit the mold rather than train workers for them. As previously mentioned, Abercrombie & Fitch wanted staff with a "preppy look" to align with their customer base and so didn't hire ethnic minority job applicants who they deemed as lacking the appropriate cultural capital.[25] Likewise, even in smaller markets like Asbury Park, employers hire already suitably skilled middle-class White students despite city leaders wanting these employers to hire unemployed local residents of color and their own progressive beliefs. Rather than taking on the racial structures and the challenges that come along with that acknowledgment, employers may prefer "plug and play" applicants capable of starting work immediately and fitting the model that is just edgy enough.

5
A West Side Story

What happened to the freedom of the water, you know?

—Latinx focus group

The beach is all White; it's like a ton of pigeons took over.

—West Side resident focus group

I have the language to respond, but my young African American male nephews really can't afford to speak back to police officers.

—Haitian American interview

We're not a great city. We don't have education. We don't have a grocery store.

—employer interview

The public school is horrible. The children is horrible.

—Latinx focus group

Gentrification is based on the destruction of a school system, and the destruction of the school system did not take place over and like that. It was a long and drawn-out process.

—activist focus group

Thus far in our journey, we have explored the experiences of individuals in the Asbury Park labor market—those working, those searching for work, and those employing workers. But what is it like to live in, to grow up in, or to raise children in Asbury Park as it experiences seasonal gentrification—particularly if one feels excluded from the new opportunities the city is offering? In this chapter, we use our ethnographic, interview, and focus group data to paint a picture of what it is like to live on the West Side of Asbury Park while the East Side prospers. We share the stories of young people and educators, with a focus on key city issues that arose as themes from our data collection and analysis, such as beach and boardwalk amenity access, over- and underpolicing, schooling, and the community supports available for children and their families. While none of these issues is unique to Asbury Park or a gentrifying community, they are heightened because of the seasonality of the gentrification and the intersections of identity in Asbury, both of which we will explore. When examining these key issues, the ongoing effects of a long history of racism in the community, the intersectionality of today's Asbury, and the burdens of seasonal gentrification are apparent. We conclude this chapter with a case study of the experiences of one man on the West Side and how his story is representative of so many of the refrains throughout the book.

Beach Access and the Boardwalk

Of all our findings, perhaps the most startling to people from outside the area is that many residents of Asbury Park's West Side, who live just about a mile from the beach, do not go to the beach. Repeatedly during our research, we heard from West Siders for whom the beach and boardwalk are not part of their lived experience despite the fact that they are the amenities to which seasonal gentrifiers are drawn. This finding was triangulated by researcher Alicia Raia-Hawrylak, who studied youth experiences in Asbury Park, where she had been a teacher. She writes in her article "Youth Experience of Space in a Gentrifying Community" about how her students, and later her research subjects, did not enjoy the boardwalk and beach and often complained of being bored. Beyond being bored, the tourism and event focus in the community seemed to have adverse effects on their neighborhood. She was surprised that her students did not attend free fireworks on the beach; instead, they told her that during those fireworks shows, their neighborhood on the West Side became more dangerous because of the protection provided at the beach.[1]

So why would residents who live so close to an amenity that others travel long distances to experience not take advantage of it? West Siders provide a variety of explanations for not using the beach regularly. The main reason given is the expense; they must pay to park and to access the beach. New Jersey is the only state in the United States in which individual beachgoers must pay for a badge to enter the beach during the day.[2] A few Jersey Shore beach towns do not charge for access, but Asbury Park does. The profits are used to fund beach upkeep. A statute allows towns to either charge no one for the beach or to charge residents with exceptions for certain allowable categories to be discounted (such as children or veterans).

While we never heard this in our interviews and focus groups, the beach in Asbury Park is technically free for children age twelve and under. However, it is not free for their parents, nor is it free for teenagers, who are undeniably in need of free or low-cost entertainment. While we were in Asbury, the cost for the beach was $5 a day during the week and $7 a day on weekends, or $70 for the season ($20 for the season for teenagers and seniors).[3] Having to pay to access the beach is a clear example of how seasonal gentrification influences the experiences of young people. This is akin to local parents in a gentrifying community having to pay to bring their children to public parks, which would affect not just their access but their relationship with the community.

Parking by the beach is also difficult to find at peak times. And regardless of the time, it costs to park a car close to the beach. During peak season, the rate is $2 an hour, and parking mechanisms increasingly rely on smartphone apps to issue payment. One Haitian American woman who grew up in Asbury laments that the parking meters do not give change: "I put a $20 in once for two-hour parking, and it does not give you change. I did not read the fine print, and the machine does not give you change."[4] As residents in our Latinx focus group say,

PARTICIPANT 1: It used to be free, but now all of a sudden, you gotta pay like seven dollars each person just to go in the water.

FACILITATOR: Right.

PARTICIPANT 1: So now you gotta find out how you can sneak in there.

FACILITATOR: Yeah.

PARTICIPANT 1: What happened to the freedom of the water, you know?

One resident explains her reasoning for not going: "If you have a lot of kids, and each one is seven dollars . . ."

As a work-around, West Side adults young and old go to the beach after hours, when it is free. One resident shares, "I don't wanna go during the time they're charging. So I go like before or after. I don't want to pay five, ten dollars." This sentiment is echoed in one of our focus group exchanges:

FACILITATOR: Do you and your children, if you have them, go to the beach? Do you go to the beach?

PARTICIPANT 1: I don't go to the beach.

PARTICIPANT 2: Yeah.

FACILITATOR: You never go to the beach?

PARTICIPANT 1: I don't like the heat, and I refuse to pay those parking meters. That's just not for me.

PARTICIPANT 2: It's expensive.

FACILITATOR: What about beach passes; you ever buy a beach pass?

PARTICIPANT 2: No.

PARTICIPANT 1: I don't do the beach at all.

PARTICIPANT 2: If I were to be, it's after 5:00.

PARTICIPANT 3: Yeah, that's when a lot of us go 'cause it's free. I mean . . .

FACILITATOR: Do you swim? Do you just hang out on the beach?

PARTICIPANT 2: Get my feet wet.

However, the very significant issue with this strategy is that lifeguards are not on duty during these off-hours, and it is dangerous—even more so if the residents have not had the opportunity to learn how to swim. School officials we spoke with discussed the drowning of a student, and this tragic story line reappears in a local news article about a man (Mr. Lyons) who drowned attempting to rescue a thirteen-year-old: "Mr. Lyons went into the water [to reach the thirteen-year-old] about 6:30 p.m., after lifeguards went off duty at 5 p.m. Mr. Lyons was taken to Jersey Shore University Medical Center in Neptune, where he was pronounced dead. Inspector Giberson said more people have been coming to the beach for relief from the heat after lifeguards are off duty, and some do not know how to swim."[5] A story about another drowning states, "The 23-year-old was last seen swimming about two blocks south after lifeguards went off duty Tuesday night."[6]

There are strong racial and socioeconomic disparities when it comes to swimming ability, further complicating beach access and safety. According to the USA Swimming Foundation, 64 percent of African American children have low/no swimming ability (compared to 45 percent of Hispanic and 40 percent of Caucasian children). In low-income families, 79 percent of children have low/no swimming ability. African American children and their families were also found to be three times more afraid of drowning than White children and their families, which is not irrational considering that according to the Centers for Disease Control and Prevention (CDC), African American children ages five to fourteen are in fact three times more likely to drown than White children.[7]

A school official explains that he or she thinks efforts have been made and that "the kids know the East Side more now. They are more comfortable on the East Side now than [in] previous years.

They plan trips to the beach, and older kids work there. They do trips to [the] splash park, mini golf, and so on. Some of the students didn't feel welcome, but the adult supervisors intervened and helped. They have started swim programs for preschool and kindergarteners to teach them how to swim. But African Americans tend to go to the beach after 4:00 p.m., when you don't have to pay—the boardwalk looks different in the day than evening."

A Haitian American woman who grew up on the East Side, demonstrating the intersectionality discussed in chapter 2, explains that while she did, and still does, feel comfortable at the beach, she understands how historically, other Black residents might not have shared her viewpoint:

Because I grew up blocks away from the beach, I felt comfortable there, but I can see how that might not be true for people from the West Side. That's how we just spent summers. It never occurred to me. But the immigrant experience is different from the African American experience. Their parents may have passed on their experiences, and history and "don't go there." I didn't come with that or have that baggage. Not to negate their experiences or feelings, but that may be why. I will do things other people of color who are African American won't, but I understand why. . . . Post-traumatic stress is real. It is real.

While learning to swim and accessing a local amenity are important, there are also stores, restaurants, activities, and job opportunities on the boardwalk and beach. We found that for most adult West Siders, accessing popular amenities on the East Side was not part of their daily lives. When we asked focus group participants if they had been to a show at the famous Stone Pony or eaten at East Side restaurants, our questions were met with silence. The reasons for this included the expense and racism by those at and on the boardwalk but also the presence of law enforcement officials and an overall lack of interest.

It makes sense that West Side residents don't feel wholly comfortable accessing the amenities on the East Side. Discrimination against Black individuals while shopping has been studied.[8] Marketplace discrimination and consumer racial profiling are real. The phrases *driving while Black* and *shopping while Black* stem from the subtle and unsubtle ways Black Americans are discriminated against while doing what others do freely. One resident explains "not feeling welcomed. Just like going up to one of the stores on the boardwalk, they'll kind of just look at you funny like, 'Why are you in here?' Even the restaurants that are on Cookman."

One local activist of color describes to another White activist focus group member that her suggestion that young people should not walk around looking for jobs together could be construed as racist: "You can go through Ocean Grove, and you can see five White guys standing together on the boardwalk, and nobody will feel bad about it. But you take five Black kids and you put them in Ocean Grove standing on the boardwalk . . . that's a gang." The White activist explains that she does not think it is smart for any group of young people to go looking for jobs together, leading the local to rebut, "That perception is a harmful perception because a lot of times these kids travel in groups. They travel in groups because it's safe." Thus while for teenagers of color, it might feel more comfortable to travel in a group, this is then perceived as a threat by others in the community. Elijah Anderson writes of the street codes that informally govern the lives of urban youth and how living in this environment can be linked to violent behavior and result in cultural adaptations differing from that of accepted, White, middle-class norms.[9]

As is often the case in gentrifying communities, the amenities that have come to support the gentrifiers are not affordable or necessary for longtime, year-round residents. Sharon Zukin encounters this in New York City: "New stores and new people produce new urban terroirs, localities with a specific cultural product and character that can be marketed around the world, drawing tourists and investors and making the city safe, though not cheap, for the middle class."[10] This is also seen in Asbury Park. As one West Sider explains, the food on the East Side is "too expensive. Like this sandwich . . . if you go on that side over there for a sandwich like this, they charging you about a six, seven dollars for just a sandwich like this . . . I can go home and make that." Meanwhile, there are no major grocery stores in Asbury Park. This area, known for its culinary feats, is a food desert for low-income residents on the West Side. While writing this book, we encountered many middle- and upper-middle-class professionals from northern New Jersey, New York, and even Los Angeles who traveled to Asbury Park for weddings, work events, vacations, or dance competitions, and the "good restaurants" in Asbury Park were cited as appealing features. At the same time, we heard about the lack of supermarkets (except for the Super Supermarket, which residents do not feel is a good and affordable option) for residents and the barriers officials have faced in trying to bring one into town.

A local activist in the nonprofit sector explains, "A West Side resident is going to spend part of their money on transportation, that money is going to go to a taxi cab driver to take them to Shop Rite, to shop and then come back. Because it's an urban food desert, and there's no supermarket within walking distance. So if they have an available transportation dollar, it's likely going to go for them to get food to bring back to their family as opposed to get them to a job, which is not within walking or biking distance." And as one Asbury Park resident puts it, "Asbury Park today is a pit bull about to pop. . . . The West Side, there's a 6–11 and no grocery and an Indian guy who will sell you loosies and rolling paper. Over here [on the East Side, there is] fancy water with olives. How apropos is that in one square mile?"

While all reasons for discomfort and barriers to using the beach and amenities on the East Side are valid and demonstrate the realities for, and perceptions of, some individuals, not all the explanations we encountered seemed wholly accurate upon further research. For example, no West Side resident, in discussing the expense of using the beach, mentioned that young children were free. We never heard about (or perhaps residents did not know about) free beach passes funded through a local GoFundMe created by an East Side resident. We heard that they had left-over beach badges from this effort that they were attempting to distribute them to seniors and parents in Asbury Park. We heard about how "all of a sudden" there was a charge for beach access, but beaches have been charging in New Jersey since a heat wave in 1929 led to crowded beaches and a desire to keep the masses out of Bradley Beach, paving the way for the other towns to implement badges.[11] When we walked on the Asbury beach on hot summer days, it was not as though all White "pigeons took over." There were many families of color and multigenerational groups with children playing in the sand speaking Spanish. When we looked at the photographs we had taken on a crowded summer afternoon, they revealed an incredibly racially diverse mix of people, including many Black beachgoers. When we walked on the boardwalk and into the popular Asbury Hotel, we saw young people of color working throughout the hotel and playing pool in the lobby. At the splash pad on a hot July day, we observed a number of Black and Brown children and families.

Living on the West Side too often means that one is living with the racial and class baggage of Asbury's past while struggling with the current seasonal gentrification. Indeed, the stories we heard from many longtime older residents on the West Side are very much rooted in both historical and present-day structural realities and racism. As Councilwoman Clayton explains, "There's still reluctance; there is still the impression 'They don't want us over there.' It's partially historical, and that is reinforced when you go to a store and feel followed." This demonstrated for us the Thomas theorem, a sociological theory that posits that situations and facts like these, which are defined as real, are in fact only real in their consequences.[12] In other words, if many parents on the West Side believe the beach to be an unwelcoming, all-White, and racist space, then this is real in its consequences. This family will then choose not to access the beach. One activist who is a woman of color says, "Some of it has been self-imposed because there was a history when Black people could not cross over . . . [the] level of comfort has to be fostered on both sides. You get a lot of 'They don't want us over there anyway.' How do you know unless you try?" Yet it is easy to see how these feelings are difficult to overcome

FIG. 14. Asbury splash park. Photograph by Molly Vollman Makris, July 21, 2019.

and have larger impacts regarding employment, particularly when residents face racist treatment and are fearful of the police.

The racial history that residents bear and the structural inequities that are felt in many gentrifying communities are exacerbated by seasonal gentrification, which has resulted in the growth of industries and amenities that cater specifically to tourists and those with disposable income for vacationing but may not be invested in living (and grocery shopping) in the community fifty-two weeks a year.

Policing and Crime

While we were conducting our research, the deaths of Philando Castile, Michael Brown, Tamir Rice, Eric Garner, and too many others were on the minds of many residents. The relationship between urban communities and the police force is fraught and complex, and this is evident in our findings and again highlights the intersectionality at play. We heard from African American West Side residents about overpolicing and from Latinx focus group participants about the need for more policing. We heard concerns from West Siders about raising children in the community and the high crime rate. We heard that the East Side was overpoliced for people of color but underpoliced for the hard-partying Jersey Shore crowd. One participant laments, "There's no happy medium . . . too aggressive, too laid back."

Parents of color expressed fear for their children, particularly young men, at the hands of the police and out in the community. We also heard about a shift in the relationship between police and the community. In the era when outsiders feared Asbury Park, residents themselves seemed to have had better experiences with the police (as detailed in chapter 2), but today, parents of color are scared. One East Side mother describes her son hanging out on the East Side: "[He] goes to the arcade down there. As the parent of a Black child, you are nervous in general. There are studies of White grown males' inability to identify adolescent Black males . . . they all look like men. I don't have time for him to be seen as somebody else and do something that could physically or emotionally scar him or jade him." She continues, "[For this] to be happening in the town I grew up in is even more upsetting. There used to be a residency requirement for police officers; it made sense because they were used to the population. Now we have an explosive concoction of young White males with no exposure to Asbury Park, but [they] live on the fringes. . . . They have no knowledge of the community and preconceived notions of what our kids are going to be like." She then describes the difference on the East Side: "They do a great, great job . . . they have called me to say I left my door open. But you don't have those protections on the other side of town. . . . They give more slack to certain vehicles. They will run the plate and call and try to avoid making people uncomfortable rather than towing a car [on the East Side]."

These experiences encapsulate much of what we found about the relationship between the community and police—the under- and overpolicing and the disconnect between police officers and the local community. In an article about a city council meeting where the police's use of excessive force on a young man was discussed, Asbury Park Black Lives Matter founder Jennifer Lewinsky is quoted as saying, "Every black person in this city can tell you a story of police brutality that they have experienced or know someone has experienced . . . I can tell you ten personal experiences."[13]

Yet residents on the West Side consistently express major concerns about crime and violence. As focus group residents describe,

PARTICIPANT 1: Shooting in the daytime.
PARTICIPANT 2: Yeah, that's our problem. We always want to; we need to stop fighting.
PARTICIPANT 1: We don't fight with hands no more.
PARTICIPANT 2: They're just killing each other.

Others we spoke to reflect these same fears: "Around here is where everything's happening because you don't know when that bullet's coming through your window. . . . That's the main thing, that bullet, because the bullet have no names." They express that there are "just guns, guns everywhere" and "guns and gangs."

In addition to the violence, residents share concerns over drug sales, as one Latinx resident tells us: "Almost right in front of my house they sell drugs. You can see it in front of a cop and kids. You can see it." And in this same focus group, a woman spoke longingly of the police presence on the East Side. A small business owner reflects on this as well:

More so on this [east] side of town . . . I think there is a police presence on the other [west] side of town. They try to keep things in check. It's a whole different thing, but I mean, you know college kids coming in and drinking and getting drunk and going to the bathroom in the streets and fighting . . . that's an easy thing to solve. . . . The other side of town is more systemic. That's a cultural thing. That's, you know, you have drugs. You have gangs. You have a lot, you know, domestic violence—you have a lot of things over there [that are] a lot harder to solve.

This speaks to the complex societal issues influencing crime but also to the common and yet flawed perception that crime can be explained as part of a culture of poverty, which fails to account for poverty's systemic causes and creates a narrative of individual and cultural blame.

A local activist explains why gangs have found a place in the community and how this is not understood well beyond the community:

> So now survival is a very, very important aspect of that child's life. You get one to walk down the street by himself, he's beat, but if you get five kids walking down the street by themselves, at least that's protection, and that's how gangs became important. I know this takes you off for a minute, but I had a kid—well, I had many kids . . . with parents, brothers, and sisters who were killed—but I had a kid on my basketball team whose brother was killed, and when he came to games on Saturday, I asked him. I said, "Are those guys from your brother's gang?" He said, "Yeah, because that's my protection." He had to get on the bus to go to the game. You know what? I said, "Then bring them." I said, "Are they packing?" He said, "Yeah, they packing," he said, "but that's to protect me." Now that's the loyalty of the gang toward a kid, OK? And that—and you have to see that dynamic to understand that dynamic, and that doesn't exist in the White community. That exists in the Black community, and so we say, "Why are gangs so big?" A lot of kids don't want to be in gangs, but they don't trust the police and then so they go to the Boys' Club and then that's cool when they go to the Boys' Club. We have to bring back the West Side Community Center because that's something that protects the kids, but you have to understand the dynamic of the community.

Sudhir Venkatesh discusses these dynamics in *American Project* and *Gang Leader for a Day*, in which he chronicles the underground economies and hustles of the once infamous Robert Taylor Homes in the Chicago Housing Authority. He discusses how gangs can actually create order and protection while also stoking great fear and creating problems.[14]

The feeling of inequity around crime and policing within Asbury due to seasonal gentrification is palpable. The police are seen as protecting the image of the East Side and the tourists so as to protect housing values. One focus group participant notes, "Well, it's legit. Crime went down. The police on that side of town, they are there in force, OK? Here, they are not here to enforce but to eradicate—eradicate whoever it is they see as a threat to the production of Asbury Park." His phrase, "the production of Asbury Park," aptly sums up the view we heard again and again—namely, that the growth and development in Asbury have been unequal and are not meant to benefit all residents. Participants recount their experiences at the hands of the police:

PARTICIPANT 1: Mind you, I was on that side at 11:00—no, I'm sorry, it was 12:00 at night—and I had picked up my grandchildren, and I was coming right on Cookman. I was making a left on Cookman, and the people were coming out of the clubs drunk and so forth. No cops standing by to police them. One ran into the back of me, pulled off. I called the police. He said, "Did you get a plate number?" I said, "No." I said, "How can I get a plate number and he ran in the back of me and pulled off?" [The officer said,] "Well, then, you'll have to see if you can find the car." Now mind you, my car is a hooptie. It's not really that expensive as the cars that were down there. Did you know he asked me, "What are you doing down here? Do you mind if I search your car? Have you been drinking?"

FACILITATOR: Did you get searched?

PARTICIPANT 1: Yes. I told him, "Yes, go ahead." He said, "Have you been drinking?" But you see, that's how it is for us.

PARTICIPANT 2: Every day.

Another describes working on cars at his home:

At my place, my driveway, where I live and pay rent. I had the car parked in front of my driveway. Do you believe a cop pulled up, threw his lights on? Now me and my family are all out there. Sometimes they sit with me while I'm working on cars. He pulled up behind me and he said, "This is illegal parking." I said, "How?" I said, "This is my driveway." [He said,] "Let me see your license and insurance and stuff." I gave it to him. He said, "Well, I'm gonna give you a ticket for illegal parking." I said, "How is that when it's right here in front of my house?" I go to court. You know when I went to court, the judge said to me, "Well, we're gonna postpone it until the twenty-first." I said, "Why?" I said, "I was on my property, where I pay rent, and I was working on a car, and I told the officer, you know, I'm working on the car, and he said it was illegal parking." He said, "Well, we'll discuss that on the twenty-first." Why couldn't it be handled right there? Do you understand what I'm saying?

Yet another interviewee of color tells us about being policed on the boardwalk:

I remember one time my nephews were riding bicycles, and the police officer stopped and [was] ready to arrest them for riding their bikes on the boardwalk, and yet all these White people were doing it, and they [my nephews] couldn't understand why they couldn't and White people could. So next time I was home, I went with them [to the police station] to see and I said, "How come my nephews can't ride their bikes and all these White people can?" [The officer said,] "Ma'am, I didn't see it." I showed them a picture I took, [and the officer said,] "Ma'am, we can't leave our spot to go after that person." But for my nephew, they could chase him.

A Latinx focus group resident described that when her son was being harassed, she called the police, but the police did not respond. Yet other locals told us that there is not overpolicing of the West Side and that they have heard the people who do not want to be seen by police are the ones who say there is overpolicing. One local man of color stipulates that this problem is not a simple matter of over- or underpolicing: "Too much or too little policing depends on which police crew—like if it's the CRAB crew of police, the 'Caucasian Race against Blacks.'"

The relationship between the community and the police is a difficult one in communities of color. Residents carry with them a long history of complicated and negative relationships with police rooted in racial inequality. In addition, concerns about the political environment for immigrants (e.g., ICE raids under the Trump administration) have created additional racial and ethnic components and further complicate this relationship. Add to this the seasonal gentrification in Asbury Park. There are areas of the community and times of the year that are heavily policed, and certain people are protected and prioritized while others in the city are perceived as threats to the "production of Asbury Park."

Education

The intersection of seasonal gentrification and education is another theme that arose from our data collection. Education is a complicated story in Asbury Park. It is a story about the district's reputation and perception, school choice, funding, demographics, inequities, and support for public schools. The education system in Asbury Park is perceived as subpar by many. We met no residents who told us they were completely happy with the school system overall. It is a public school system that is consistently ranked low. Although the measures of school quality based in large part on standardized tests are flawed and give a better account of demographics than the culture and learning inside a school, they *are* frequently cited and oft looked at by parents, community members, and the general public. According to a new public school score in New Jersey in 2018 (which gives a number based on factors such as Partnership for Assessment of Readiness for College and Careers [PARCC] proficiencies, graduation rates, and chronic absenteeism), Asbury Park High School was in the fifth percentile with a score of 8.8 out of 100. The three elementary schools ranged from 1.6 to 8.8 out of 100 and from zero to the eleventh percentile.[15]

Asbury Park High School, the only district high school (with an enrollment of 402 students), is hypersegregated, with 98 percent of students identifying as Black/Latino. In the 2017–2018 school year, the student body was 64 percent Black / African American and 34 percent Hispanic. Out of all students, 20 percent had disabilities, 17 percent were English-language learners, and 43 percent were socioeconomically disadvantaged.[16] This socioeconomically disadvantaged number is likely an underestimate due to the Community Eligibility Provision (CEP) that was phased in after the 2014–2015 school year, making it more difficult to accurately report free and reduced lunch qualification.[17] In 2015–2016, 86.8 percent of students in the high school were reported as socioeconomically disadvantaged, which is likely a better estimate. Of home languages spoken, 24.9 percent of students spoke Spanish, and 15.2 percent spoke Haitian. The chronic absenteeism rate is 35.4 percent compared to the state average of 14.9 percent. Of graduates, 53.2 percent enrolled in college compared to a state average of 77.9 percent. In assessments, 21.8 percent of students met or exceeded standards in English language arts (ELA), and 14.2 percent met or exceeded standards in math.[18]

Residents repeatedly voiced their concerns about the education and safety in the schools. Residents from the West Side who grew up in the Asbury school system express that their educational backgrounds are an impediment to employment. One states, "I worked in . . . landscaping, construction, gutting houses out, housekeeping, and fast food—you know, working with elderly people. . . . So I got mad, I got a lot . . . I ain't gonna say 'mad skills' because it doesn't sound right, but I got a lot of skills. But I don't have the education. The education I have is just eighth grade only." As a local small business owner says, "The fact that we have such a horrible school district down here is a huge problem," and a Latina focus group participant describes the public school as "horrible."

Residents and school advocates do at times point to successes and argue that the school district is improving and merely suffers from a false reputation. Deputy mayor of Asbury Park, Amy Quinn, who began sending her young child to the Asbury Park public preschool, is incredibly happy with her decision and with the school community of which he is a part. In conversations with us, she praises the innovative curriculum and hopes to see other middle-class professionals make this same choice to opt in.

While conducting our research, the superintendent of Asbury Park schools, Lamont Rapollet, was selected as the New Jersey commissioner of education, with a number of outlets and locals praising the improvements in Asbury under his watch.[19] We heard about a boys' lacrosse team, golf, the hip-hop academy, rising PARCC scores, championship sports teams, and a partnership with Brookdale Community College. Yet tellingly, we also often heard about how *even the school board members* do not send their children to the public schools in Asbury Park. Yet school advocates point to perception as part of the problem and argue that White residents do not understand the good things that are happening. One activist explains, "When I told somebody that Asbury's kids go to Harvard, they were like, 'What?' That's not the perception that you have, so we have to change that perception, and that's hard to do, you know, because there are prejudices that are already out there, and people tend to want to protect their children." Media representations of a failing school district do not help when advocates are looking to improve the schools, foster buy-in, and support the children and families using these schools.

In addition, factors outside the classroom are affecting young people in school. Hunger, allostatic load, residential segregation, racism, the necessity of work, caretaking responsibilities, special educational needs, summer learning loss, health disparities, trauma, language barriers, and single parenting can all influence a student's educational outcomes.[20] As Jean Anyon explains in *Ghetto Schooling*, "Attempting to fix inner-city schools without fixing the city in which they are embedded is like trying to clean the air on one side of a screen door."[21] As one Asbury Park activist says, "We can't send them home 'cause either there's nobody home or their parents have lived in this worn-down, war-torn West Side of Asbury

Park for forty years, and their parents have no hope. You could walk down Springwood Avenue and cut the depression sometimes with a knife. I mean, maybe you can't, but I feel it. So where do we send our kids? Where—how do we find ways to work with the young people so they can begin to have some kind of hope in their world?" We also heard multiple times that parent involvement is perceived to be a huge struggle for the schools.

While the Asbury Park school system may seem to be another example of the unfortunately typical story of subpar urban education and hypersegregation, the story of education in Asbury Park is also more complicated with seasonal gentrification. While gentrification and education is a growing field of scholarship, we have seen no research on seasonal gentrification and education. Prior education research on gentrification more generally shows that education in most gentrifying communities does not improve schools or shift the demographics of local district schools in ways that benefit long-term residents. While some schools do experience gentrifiers who "opt in," in these cases, the culture, demographics, and support generally shift to support the middle-class White populations.[22] Yet generally, as Nicole Hannah-Jones argues, gentrification stops at the schoolhouse door.[23] A variety of school policies and choices—from charter and magnet schools, to gifted and talented programs, and specialized admissions schools—result in between- and within-school segregation.[24]

Yet there is some promising evidence in Washington, DC, that gentrification could hold hope for desegregation.[25] As more middle-class families choose to stay in cities, we are experiencing a moment in which residential segregation historically tied to school segregation is shifting, and as neighborhoods diversify, so potentially could their schools. In Asbury, it appears that many residents would like to see newcomers opt in to schooling to shift the perception, demographics, and resources, but this is not happening in any significant numbers and is impeded by the fact that many middle-class and new gentrifiers are seasonal and not sending their children to school in Asbury.

School choice further complicated this potential in Asbury. Historically and contemporarily, those with the capital to negotiate school choice have benefited. Asbury Park is no exception; school choice is used by those with capital in the city to avoid the district public schools. Catholic schools have been a popular choice for many and still are. Additionally, for those who know how to navigate the charter choice system, there are now two charter schools in Asbury Park: Hope Academy and College Achieve Greater Asbury (and nearby, Academy Charter High School). Interdistrict choice is also used by families to send their children to schools in the nearby town of Deal. Deal has an interdistrict choice system, which allows out-of-district families that apply and win a lottery to send their children to Deal's elementary school tuition-free and with transportation. Deal has allowed for this in an effort to maintain a school system in this small, wealthy beachfront enclave. Deal Elementary is 74 percent White and 3 percent Asian, with 0 percent English-language learners and 14 percent students with disabilities. For high school, selective county schools are sought as alternatives to Asbury Park High School or costly private schools.[26] High Technology High School in Monmouth County is consistently ranked well. Its demographics contrast startlingly with Asbury Park High School. High Technology is 53.5 percent Asian, 40.2 percent White, 2.4 percent Hispanic, 2.4 percent Black / African American, and 2.4 percent Hispanic. Students with disabilities represent 0 percent, and 2.8 percent of students are socioeconomically disadvantaged. At High Technology High School, 98 percent of students met or exceeded the ELA standards, and 96.8 percent met or exceeded the math standards.[27] In this way, school choice is an obstacle to middle-class families— and all those with the ability to negotiate choice (no language barriers, social networks that inform them, means to research and apply)—opting in to Asbury schools.

Despite its reputation, one piece of the Asbury school story that came up frequently was that the district schools are perceived as very well funded and are often covered in the media this way (over $30,000 per pupil and double the state average),[28] but this is deceiving. This funding is not so high when one considers the educational needs of a student body that is predominantly socioeconomically disadvantaged. However, on the surface, press coverage creates the perception of high funding. As one activist explains, the money and even strong school leadership are not enough:

I think we have to have more systemic approaches because, you know . . . the truth is, our high school . . . I think each kid gets $32,000 a year, which is more than most. So it's not even like kids aren't getting money in the high school; it's that you can't just have a new superintendent—who is, like, pretty great, but I haven't really been around any other ones, but it seems like he's trying. You can't just trust him to do it. It's like you know if housing is bad, the business system is extremely racist and classist, and a lot of parents aren't there—you know if we're not talking about what is actually causing people [whose] . . . parents also didn't have good education. It's not cement how ghettos were created based off of slavery and not being able to pass equity.

In fact, the school system in Asbury is seen as so flawed, expensive, and underutilized that it was not uncommon to hear residents and others mention getting rid of the district schools in Asbury Park altogether: "You know what? We'd be better if these kids went somewhere else. It's honestly—I don't wanna . . . public school's a great thing, but I don't care where my kid goes to school. I just want her to get the best-quality education."

Yet in Asbury, where the gentrification is seasonal and the community intersectional, the dynamics are again additionally complex. There are criticisms that gentrifiers, LGBTQ community members, and those in power are not focused on making Asbury Park a better community for children because children are considered to be a low priority to these constituencies. When outsiders are investing in the community for seasonal or investment property use, they are less connected to institutions such as schools and, some would argue, less inclined to want to pay higher taxes to support these institutions. As one activist explains, "There was questions about whether or not they were trying to close the school district down or something like that, and somebody who was in the position—I want to say it was on city council, I don't know—but [they] were asked, you know, 'Well, what are we going to do about this?' And the response was, 'We're not trying to attract people here that have children.' That was a real answer." We heard from residents that gentrifiers in Asbury Park, particularly gay men, were not planning to have families in the local schools and thus did not support the schools. While it is common in gentrifying communities to hear about early gentrifiers being young couples who move away when they have school-aged children, in many gentrifying communities, this narrative has begun to shift as the cities experience family gentrification and reurbanization, and city neighborhoods become more family friendly, with increasing numbers of middle-class parents choosing to stay and raise families. However, in Asbury, there is a strong feeling that children, and local families with children in the schools, are in no way a priority because they are not a key demographic in seasonal Asbury Park.

The fact that developers can point to the perceived overfunding of Asbury Schools has allowed them, as major players in the gentrifying community, and others to avoid investing further in the school system. One developer, using the kind of market-based language around education common among those in private industry, says, "Schools get a lot of funding; [the district] doesn't want for money." He continues, "Do we have a money issue or a management issue in schools? It's how we're spending the dollars. Asbury Park—there are those who say they need more. Kids don't get services they need at home." According to the waterfront developer agreement, iStar is not required to pay taxes but must pay a PILOT (payment in lieu of taxes) instead, so the funding from this development does not benefit the school system at all (versus a normal tax situation, wherein 50 percent might benefit the schools). In a seasonally gentrifying community, the voices in support of the school system are also dampened because the powerful families with middle-class social and cultural capital are not parents in the district with a personal stake in fighting against agreements that stand to undermine the educational experiences of their children and the politicians who support them. In a district with developer interests and a predominantly low-income student body, there is less broad political capital for the schools.

As is often the case, the fight concerning choice and charter schools in Asbury Park is caught up in larger neoliberal policy discussions of privatization, school funding, and tenure and teacher protections. One charter parent explains her thinking: "The charter school coming to town made the school rise up, made the board of education better and more progressive, led to hiring better administrators. There was a lot of apathy in the district. I think they get way too much funding for the results they are getting—apathetic tenured teachers . . . tenure is a joke to me. Why should my kids have to live with a person who is boss no matter what? I've always been a proponent of public schools." This parent goes on to make a connection between gentrification and schools of choice as seen in other gentrifying neighborhoods: "There are more families coming and staying, and I am hoping this [new] charter starts that process so the younger hipsters don't move out, and then eventually, [their children] will move into the public school system.'" Here she speaks to a trend that has been seen in other New Jersey communities and beyond, where charter schools can provide a seemingly parallel public system that is attractive to gentrifier parents who want to stay in the community but do not feel comfortable with the district schools.[29] This is another way that communities can diversify without their district school demographics shifting. However, district advocates argue that these charter schools drain needed resources from the district and are not much better for students. As one public school advocate explains, "The new charter that wants to open—I would support it if it was better for students, but it's not historically a great charter school. Charters have a cushion of a couple of years. They take money from the district and can send the worst kids back."

Small business owners and developers frequently lament the school funding and complain about the district school system in general. They show support for options outside of the traditional district, demonstrating again the not-infrequent connection among business, private interest, and neoliberal education reform that is seen outside of Asbury Park.[30] Connections between developers and schools are not uncommon.[31] Developers will support schools such as charter schools, early childhood programs, and private day-cares and private schools in an attempt to increase local property values.[32] A small business owner in Asbury Park who is involved in development explains his support of a new charter: "They just got the charter, but they're trying to find property right now. So we're trying to help them find property, and this [charter leader] guy's been great. He's like done a lot of it on the West Coast."

And yet even within a district that has a majority of minority students and below-average test scores, we heard about inequities between schools. As one activist explains, "The one in worst condition—you can drive by and see people dumping mattresses and stuff—is called Obama School. The other ones, the parents are homeowners, longtime renters, stable jobs. Obama pulls from the projects . . . Obama traditionally has all the worst things—gym floor terrible, low maintenance." In 2019, it was announced that Asbury would lose $24 million in state aid, and a plan was made to shut down the Obama School.

Clearly, seasonal gentrification influences the education of young people in ways that are similar to and different from gentrification in other communities. Asbury schools are faced with developer interests, neoliberal school choice, and inequities between schools, but in a seasonally gentrifying community, the vast majority of newcomers are not considering raising children in the community. Newcomers and tourists do not have much contact with those who actually utilize the schools, and school demographics do not shift. This influences the perception of schools, support for funding/taxes, political capital for schools, and resources for children. Developers—a hugely powerful force in any gentrifying community—and business interests use low rankings, high funding, and lack of buy-in to their advantage, and local parents have little capital to fight this. With accusations of underperforming, overfunding, loss of funding, safety concerns, school closures and threats of closures, increasing charter sector competition, and a community changing rapidly outside the school walls, it is understandable that residents see gentrification as a threat to local education. As one activist explains, "Gentrification is based on the destruction of a school system, and the destruction of the school system did not take place over and like that. It was a long and drawn-out process."

Children "Breaking into Play": An Adult Playground

Living in Asbury Park as it undergoes seasonal gentrification raises additional questions for those with families. An ongoing complaint that arose during our research is that because of its seasonal gentrification, Asbury Park is not a family-friendly community; instead, it is an "adult paradise" or "adult playground." Residents frequently lamented the lack of after-school, weekend, and summer activities for youth as well as adequate free green space and play areas. We heard repeatedly about the closure of the West Side Community Center and other places for young people. As a focus group participant explains, "Mostly they don't have nothing for the kids to do productive around here. You know they closed the West Side [Community Center] down. I mean, when I was growing up, I mean, in Asbury Park, you had so much to do." One school advocate even suggests that young people feel they have to break the law to play: "There is nothing for them to do. Bradley has a soccer field, but it locks at dusk. They cut the fence and get in, and neighbors get mad. But this is a symptom. There is a need. Breaking in to play!" She continues, "We are small and landlocked; the free land is not being allocated toward anything like that. They want more development, but there is no free play area."

This is where seasonal gentrification again complicates the story. While in other cities, developers might be seeking to bring in wealthy families who invest in a gentrifying community (and larger properties), in Asbury, new development is aimed at a different market.[33] As the boardwalk redevelops, it is not activities aimed at children and families that are rapidly expanding; the carousel of yesteryear has not returned to the boardwalk. As a local activist in the nonprofit sector explains, "I don't think their [developers'] target market and their interested buyers are families. You can look at any number of factors that indicate that. Price points are one. Just look at the boardwalk, by the way, compared to the boardwalk in the 1940s, '50s, and '60s. It's not a family environment. Every business up there is connected to food or alcohol— every business. That's not going to attract a year-round purchaser who has a family." The population of children in Asbury Park is decreasing; children nineteen and under composed 32.6 percent of the city population in the 2000 Census but just 25.3 percent of the city population by 2017.[34] Since most seasonal gentrifiers who visit with children buy beach passes, they can use the two playgrounds on the beach and thus are not likely to advocate for playgrounds, open play space, and other child-friendly spaces elsewhere in town. Meanwhile, more recent adult seasonal gentrifiers who have come to love the hipster-quirky charm of Asbury say they do not want to see it cluttered with boardwalk rides like other Jersey Shore towns. Yet these rides and amusements (if affordable/accessible) might provide some amenities for children in the community and were historically part of the Asbury experience.

While children from New York City, New Jersey, and elsewhere visit Asbury to play on the beach and splash in the hotel pools, there is not an abundance of open play space for local children even as hotels and other amenities are growing for the seasonal gentrifiers. There are no public outdoor swimming pools in Asbury Park, and hotel pools are not open to the public. However, at the trendy Asbury Hotel, we did observe youth coming in to play billiards in the publicly accessible lobby. Hotels like the Asbury do try on occasion to open their spaces to the public and have offerings such as free skating lessons and craft markets. We heard about a local group that offers free surf lessons, yet we also heard that recruiting from the West Side can be a challenge, and this leaves some on the East Side under the impression that West Side youth may be uninterested because they have "never been exposed to water." As one developer says while also subtly referencing the West Side buying in to programs like these, "I have huge amounts of compassion, but you've got to want it."

We heard about a park called Library Park that local government officials "tried to underhandedly turn into a dog park." This is an issue in many gentrifying communities, leading some journalists and academics to discuss whether dog parks are exclusionary.[35] Derek Hyra writes about how dog parks are given preference over other amenities in the Shaw / U-Street Community of Washington, DC—a move that was supported predominantly by the White middle-class gentrifiers. These policies can lead to the alienation of and resentment from longtime residents of color.[36] We also heard about a splash pad that was shuttered on the West Side while a new one was opened (at a cost for admission) on the East Side. The splash pad on the boardwalk is $10 per child and $5 per adult during the week and $12 and $6, respectively, on weekends. Yet when we asked around about this, we were told that the splash pad on Bangs Avenue on the West Side was very much still open.

Residents reflect on the connection between a lack of summer activities and employment and issues with youth: "If you don't give our kids something to do, what do you think they're going to do? We need to turn this stuff around to the point where your kid, my kid can . . . go to summer camp—somewhere where they can get a summer job in their own town." One local activist explains that he does not think the city supports activities for the youth:

But here's the thing, right? They made $4.5 million on parking last year, right? . . . And [the recreation for Asbury youth] . . . at the West Side Community Center and the center court—we can't get a sponsorship from Asbury Park. We can't get a basketball. We can't get none of this, and you want to know why we're frustrated? You want to know why some people do what they do? So understand, but then when you ask our kids, "What kind of work do you want to do?" they're clueless, you know what I'm saying? Most of them drop out. Most of them come out to the street, and you'll see them. When they get out there, they get angry, and they're angry at the wrong people, honestly.

Summer in this summer city can be particularly difficult for local parents who cannot afford expensive camps. As one Latina focus group participant tells us, "My youngest daughter, she don't have nothing because they don't have anything out here, and you have to pay for it and . . . being that I'm on a budget, you know what I'm saying? I can't afford it, you know?" A Jersey Shore half-day summer surf camp would be between $300 and $400 a week, and New Jersey families of means even send their children to sleep-away camps costing about $9,000 to $14,000 for the summer. The City Recreation Department and the Board of Education do collaborate with local sponsors on a summer recreation program that offers a full day of activities and trips and enrichment and meals, but we did not hear about this from families on the West Side, again demonstrating a disconnect.

Elijah

We met Elijah one boiling-hot afternoon in Asbury Park in the summer of 2018. We walked into a local nonprofit we had been working with to see if they could locate an adult male who might be willing to talk to us in depth about his experiences in Asbury Park. At that moment, Elijah, a youthful-looking twenty-year-old African American man, was sitting alone in the center on a computer checking his email and ostensibly looking for work. He was interested and very willing to speak with us. His story left us feeling equal parts heartened and disheartened.

Elijah grew up in Asbury Park with his mom, who "worked constantly," and his "Pops," who was "around—but not that much." He began his discussion with us detailing what he remembers of his educational history, which, like many in Asbury Park, was not a linear path from preschool through district high school. Elijah's education story bounces around a bit; he remembers swinging on swings at his preschool, and at some point, he ended up attending public schools outside of Asbury Park. "All these schools that's around I attended," he explains, and he spent some time in other towns and out of state but ended up always back in the area. Later he dropped out of high school. He then returned to school at Asbury Park High School, where he says the school community "accepted me for who I am," and he is incredibly proud that he recently graduated (one of his siblings also recently graduated from a charter school). He has high hopes to be a role model for children in the community.

The fits and starts and challenges he faced during his schooling are understandable when he explains, "I love school, but it's been challenges—like having to wonder how we're going to get a meal on the table for the next couple of hours. I always thought about stuff like that or 'Is my mom going to be home because she's working two or three jobs?' Trying to do the best that she can to keep the lights on and stuff like that. Hey, there are certain things that I couldn't help but to go through, but I wake up in the morning and have a smile on my face ready to start the next day." He says he got in trouble at school at times, and his school had its challenges: "Going to school was tough. You always have to defend what you know what you have to. You go to school, and you fight for your education."

Elijah has struggled to find consistent employment now that he is out of school. He says we will likely spot him around town doing odd jobs and making music and that he applies for any and all jobs. He has worked at a restaurant and Six Flags outside of Asbury Park in the past and says that Asbury Park High School helped him find employment through a summer jobs program for students. He describes how it was psychologically difficult for him working at Six Flags and coming home to the West Side: "Just having to leave and go home and just seeing a lot of families that are in New Jersey be a part of a beautiful program like Six Flags. I feel like just seeing the kids, young kids . . . the negative was just leaving. . . . It was tough because I know kids in Asbury, they look at me like, 'You, you work at Six Flags. We've never even seen Six Flags.' You know what I mean?" Now Elijah hopes to secure work doing manual labor: "I just really want to set an example for the community that there's more to do after high school. It's a challenge, it's a battle. There's life after school. Now you guys see me putting in the work trying to get a job for myself . . . I really want to do construction maybe. Boxes, I want to try to move boxes."

We asked Elijah if he knows how to swim. He tells us that he does not but says he would like to. We wanted to gauge his awareness and use of the beach and boardwalk. In this telling exchange, he says he has probably been to the beach ten times this season, but despite having always lived in the area, he has not heard about beach passes or badges:

FACILITATOR 1: Do you go during the day or at night or both?
ELIJAH: Anytime.
FACILITATOR 1: Do you have a beach badge?
ELIJAH: Oh, no, I don't know about that. I don't know about the beach badge.

He describes the challenges of growing up on the West Side and his own issues with the law, which he does not wish to go into with us much, but he shares that he has grown from and since these experiences: "It's a lot of drugs and smoking and drinking. You've got community liquor stores—thieves and stuff like that, they're around. I've done stuff too, a lot of mistakes, but now that I'm older, it's just like, 'This the older me.' When you're young, you make mistakes. Now I know, 'OK, this is how this works.' You learn and you grow, and that's what's happening to me right now." He tells us about a negative interaction he had on the East Side with police officers when he scared them (on purpose) and they handcuffed him. But he says all of his experiences with law enforcement have not been bad. He remembers one police officer who took him and his family "to a shelter home or something like that." Elijah says he would like to thank that officer if he could.

We wanted to assess whether Elijah feels he can have a political impact, and we asked him if he has voted. He tells us, "I haven't voted, but I know there's a lot of stuff going on in the presidency and stuff like that. I'm not really big on it." He does not know who the mayor of Asbury Park is: "It's a man . . . is it Chris Christie?"[37] He also says he is not sure if his family members vote: "I'm not sure on that much. I feel like we're trying to just make a way, you know what I mean?"

Despite the obstacles he has overcome, Elijah has high hopes for the future: "I can't wait to get my car and get my license. I've got my state ID; once I hit the road, I'm going to be part of the driving community and see how that goes. Hopefully I don't get no car crashes." He says he failed the tests for driver's education at the high school: "I always failed the driving thing. Hopefully I read and start to pick up that book." Further, Elijah explains to us, "I know what it feels like to be homeless and hungry." He considers his community deeply and thoughtfully and brings up an issue that was not mentioned in any of our other interviews. He is curious about the public housing projects that are now gone and asks, "What happened to people who lived there?"

As our discussion was winding down, Elijah took a call from his mother. His love for her, and hers for him, was palpable. She tells him she will drive him home and they tell each other "I love you." Elijah tells us, "Yeah, it's tough right now. My vision is to get my mom a house. It doesn't matter what the circumstances is." At the conclusion of our discussion, Elijah gave the monetary incentive we had provided him to a seven-year-old African American boy who had popped in to ask to use his headphones. Elijah told him to make sure he gets some food with the money. The seven-year-old has never been to the beach or swam, but he plays basketball. The young child then ran from the room excitedly shouting, "I made $20 bucks!" which made Elijah smile.

Despite what he has been through and the issues he encounters daily, Elijah is optimistic about the future of Asbury Park. He asks us if we have seen the new park on the West Side. He says, "Just imagine when everything's all done, it's going to be a beautiful community with lawyers and doctors and so forth and so on." But for now, he tells us of the struggle between the haves and the have-nots: "It's tough to make it across the railroad tracks because now you've got all this new stuff going on besides the apartments that they're building. It's beautiful over there by Cookman; you've got a sense of hope. Even though you've got this side and this side, you make that transition. It's just like when individuals from Cookman . . . come over here and they look at the community like, 'Oh my goodness. Wow.'"

But Elijah concludes, "It's all right, though. Asbury ten years from now is going to be a together thing."

6

Cats Are the New Dogs
(and Other Stuff That Makes
Asbury Cool . . . and Can It Stay Cool?)

So we, my husband and I, have always—that's the beach we choose to go
to. When we go to the beach, we go a couple of times every year. Not just
the beach, but the convention center comic and toy convention, punk rock
flea market. We go year-round whenever things are going on. It's an easy
drive [from northwest New Jersey]. . . . Asbury always felt more casual. I'm
super preppy and can go anywhere, but my husband is half Puerto Rican
and tattooed on his arms and would have been the object of stares and
disgruntled looks elsewhere. Asbury Park felt like a place we would both
be comfortable being. That has been the case. We're probably some of the
least quirky people on the beach there. This summer we stayed in Bradley,
but we went to Asbury every day. We took our daughter to the boardwalk. We can't afford to stay in Asbury anymore. We could have afforded
five years ago to go there. All these Hoboken people are going now. I say,
"No, not Asbury—this is my safe haven." I love walking the boardwalk and
people watching on the boardwalk. I love the murals; we go and see all
the new murals, particularly on the north end of the boardwalk they had
added a few more this year. My husband is an artist and grew up painting
murals. It's sad to see what's happening with murals on the other side. The
vision seems to be what someone has for Asbury, not what I think it should
be. I don't want it to be just another town on the shore.

—*tourist interview*

FIG. 15. Art on the East Side. Photograph by Erika Bentley Leonard, September 10, 2019.

Asbury Park is seen as undeniably cool and "impossibly hip" by many of its residents and visitors. Yet Asbury Park is also having a moment; it is perched right on the precipice of quirky coolness and bland hipster paradise, and it remains to be seen if it will be able to maintain its cool in the face of an onslaught of developers, investors, and outsiders. As we were writing this chapter, Molly sat on a panel for graduate students considering getting a PhD. One of them approached her, excited about the book, and asked if we would be writing about how "they destroyed the Lanes."

The Asbury Lanes serves as a microcosm of the larger battle taking place in Asbury Park. In many ways, it illustrates how the coolness of Asbury may be at risk, another theme that was repeated in our data collection. As John Bazley describes for the *Asbury Park Press*,

> Something you'll learn by speaking with anyone who frequented
> the Asbury Lanes is that everyone has a Lanes story, and in
> most stories, the music comes second. Yes, I saw the Menzingers
> create history at the Lanes . . . but I can't remember a single song

FIG. 16. The East Side. Photograph by Erika Bentley Leonard, September 10, 2019.

they played because I only remember my friends' faces and that forgotten feeling of being home with them. Pro wrestler CM Punk was allegedly in the venue that night. I didn't see him, but I believe that story, because I've heard it from people who knew the magic that old bowling alley created. I have no reason to doubt them.[1]

In 2015, the Asbury Lanes, a retro bowling alley featuring edgy shows and cheap food, was closed, and iStar (the developer of the Asbury Hotel, Ocean Club, etc.) made plans to reopen it. This place, once known as a vestige for punks, relaunched in 2018 and is now seen as a sold-out, rich-developer version of its former self. Bazley continues, "Gone are the paintings on the walls, the vintage décor, the support beams where every local band would slap their homemade stickers. Instead, there's a gaudy diner sign, tacky bean-bag chairs, and an aesthetic that screams that the undesirables, the punks who built this place, who only have five dollars for the show and maybe a few dollars for pizza afterward, are no longer welcome."[2]

"They turned something really cool into the Hard Rock Cafe," says Dale W. Miller, a musician whose former band, Atlantic/Pacific, played the old Asbury Lanes. He continues, "Its quirks—bands played on a stage over the lanes and people bowled in either side—were what many locals felt made it great."[3] However, not everyone is unhappy. Brian Cheripka, the senior vice president for land and development at iStar, explains in an interview with NJ.com that the new Asbury Lanes allows them to actually save the venue and triple the capacity while reusing the old lanes to create the new flooring. The Salt School (explored in chapter 4), which provides job training to locals, now places graduates at the Lanes. Bruce Springsteen played a brief set at the sold-out opening show in June 2018, and iStar donated $125,000 to the Boys & Girls Club of Monmouth County in lieu of payment to the Boss. Cheripka is the second vice president on the board of officers for the Boys & Girls Club of Monmouth County, and Bruce Springsteen is widely seen as a huge supporter and advocate of the community. This demonstrates the kind of complex neoliberal relationship web that exists in gentrifying communities among developers, local history, those with means, support for social services, and the local community.

In this chapter, using our ethnographic data along with media pieces on Asbury Park, we explore the current fashion industry, art galleries, grungy-punk tattooed tourists, and festivals that are drawing visitors and residents. We contrast this "cool Asbury" with the experiences of long-term residents of color. We also look at big developers and the real estate industry in Asbury Park, which are feeding on the city's newfound cool. Will what makes Asbury cool be figuratively and literally whitewashed away? In the end, will the quirky diversity be the downfall of the community? As one activist explains, "I think the irony is, why Asbury? It's the diversity [that has made it popular], but the economics might drive that diversity out. It won't be as cool as it once was. Its success will be the source of its undoing, maybe."

FIG. 17. Transportation sponsored by the Boss. Photograph by Erika Bentley Leonard, September 10, 2019.

In Asbury Park, there are the now typical trappings of gentrification from fusion bites and gourmet donuts to beer gardens and craft brews. There is also a coffee shop where you can snuggle adoptable cats that need homes and purchase a trendy "Catsbury Park Springsteen" T-shirt. Professionals in the fashion industry from New York City travel to Asbury for ideas. There is a zombie parade at Halloween time, a drag queen story hour for local children at the bookstore, a tattoo festival, and a Cat Convention. At a fusion taco spot, the bathroom doors and trash cans are fittingly covered in graffiti and stickers. The deputy mayor with a visible social media presence and podcast is a lesbian mama who wears her "Lesbian AF" and "Feminist AF" T-shirts with pride and sports a large feminist tattoo.

Yet not all amenities are accessible or even edgy. On one of our visits to this quirky hotspot city, a Madewell [a J.Crew chain brand] truck was parked outside the Asbury Hotel, and when we noticed $200 to $300 and up sunglasses at a local boutique, we were told they were handmade in New Orleans. The store has limited merchandise space, so owners say they "have to pick special items." A tourist who works in the fashion industry describes why designers and their teams from New York City travel to Asbury for inspiration: "Asbury Park is a great town to draw new and old inspiration from . . . there are also lots of new and emerging designers and local artisans selling in boutiques in town and on the boardwalk."

Other neighborhoods and cities that have undergone processes of urban renewal have seen a particular flavor of gentrification befitting local culture. In these cases, community culture has been turned into a commodity. Arlene Dávila writes of the Latinization and gentrification of East Harlem in New York City that has gone hand in hand with neoliberal privatization.[4] Changes to the East Village and the glamorization of poverty and grit are detailed by Christopher Mele.[5] These neighborhood changes inspired writer Jeremiah Moss to pen *Vanishing New York: How a Great City*

Lost Its Soul, which contains chapters like "Mourning the Low-Rent, Weirdo-Filled East Village of Old."[6] Sharon Zukin similarly writes of how New York has lost its soul.[7] In his best-selling book *The Rise of the Creative Class,* Richard Florida describes how a city can be economically successful by appealing to the creative class.[8] Florida has also been harshly critiqued for his views and their influence on gentrification and inequity. Asbury Park meets many of the criteria of Florida's successful cities: it is welcoming of LGBTQ residents (*tolerance* is one of the three Ts he recommends for a city's success) and has music, galleries, and outdoor activities.

While the East Side appears to be thriving—if under the constant threat of "disneyification"[9]—it is a different story for now on the West Side. A small business owner who has chosen not to locate close to the beach says, "I hear this all the time: 'Oh, well, the boardwalk is so full. You must be doing great in the middle of the summer.' No, abso-freakin'-lutely not, not at all, but if I'm not doing well, then the West Side is seeing less than nothing. What they're seeing is the blur of cars speeding past, and then again you hear the city manager [say], 'Oh, when I moved here, my mother thought I was going to be shot.'"

Small Businesses

One of the pieces of Asbury that has contributed to its rise in cachet has been the passion and ideas of small business owners. As described in chapter 4, it is evident that many of these small business owners believe deeply in the community and are invested beyond their storefronts. As Asbury gains popularity, they stand to benefit, but only if they can stay. As one small business owner says of gentrification, "It's a blessing and it's a curse."

Another owner describes the shift from those who moved to the community to contribute to those who have come to consume: "When I moved here, there were a lot of doers. Like everybody I've met was like, 'Oh, I'm an artist. I do this'; 'I'm a musician. I moved to Asbury to do this'; 'I make furniture. I moved here to do this' . . . now it's just consumers. People aren't moving here to be like, 'I have this dream, and I want to do that,' you know, and that's sort of sad for me because it's not affordable for people to do that anymore." The fashion designer tourist we interviewed mentioned that in the summer of 2019, one team she knew of was foregoing their Asbury trip because a few of their favorite stores had closed.

There is a fear, as one small business owner expresses, that what has happened in other changing communities will happen in Asbury: "[Other towns] went from mom and pop quickly to Gap and Banana Republic, and it took everything away from that town and just sucked the life out of it, and I hope that doesn't happen here." Hoboken, New Jersey, provides a startling example of this, as the main thoroughfare, Washington Street, now boasts a Sephora, Athleta, West Elm, and soon a Lululemon, while many locals feel it has lost its old-school charm. In New York City, this has advanced to the next stage. Derek Thompson describes the "rich ghost town" of Manhattan with empty storefronts in the West Village, on Fifth Avenue, and on Bleecker Street (what Tim Wu calls "high rent blight"[10]). Commercial rents have increased, online shopping has increased, and landlords would prefer to rent to national brands for long-term leases. As Thompson explains in an *Atlantic* article, "The 2018 landlord waiting game is denuding New York of its particularity and turning the city into a high-density simulacrum of the American suburb. The West Village landlords hoping to lease their spaces to national chains are turning one of America's most famous neighborhoods into a labyrinthine strip mall. Their strategy bodes the disappearance of those quirky restaurants, curious antique shops, and any coffee shops that aren't publicly traded on the NYSE."[11]

Another Asbury small business owner reports that people will come to him and ask, "What is there to do in town?" He says he tells them, "I don't know. There's nothing to do." He continues, "You know, God bless you if you're sober. Like there's nothing to do on the boardwalk besides eat or drink, and there may or may not be the one shop that's there if you want to buy, you know, an $80 pair of shorts." As Asbury Park grows and continues its seasonal gentrification, small business owners may find the independent stores they own (and that in many ways defined Asbury's coolness in the early 2000s) are increasingly at risk for displacement. This leaves many in the city—new residents, activists, and business owners alike—questioning the future of the city's cool.

Diversity Sells

Diversity is another key piece of what makes Asbury Park cool. As one small business owner explains, "I was very intrigued by the fact that [Asbury] sort of escaped the whole sort of stigma of the Jersey Shore . . . but the music, I think, is what kept it more diverse than other seaside towns in New Jersey."

The developers in the city recognize that they need to try to keep this appeal of the town alive. As a developer states, "Some places have employee rules: 'All tattoos must be covered and [no] beards.' If I was strict, I would have no employees. I love their tattoos and their hair and their differences." This attitude is evident around town, where restaurant hosts on the boardwalk are often trendy, attractive teenagers or young adults, and employees at the Asbury Hotel were often flashily dressed young people of color. A developer explains, "The word in New York hotels was *exclusive, exclusive, exclusive*. Now one of our big things is *inclusive* for staff and guests. Everyone is treated the same. On a Sunday morning, I will see young couples and White and Black and kids and dogs and surfers and watching all that go on." Dog lovers are welcome to Yappy Hour at Wonder Bar and quirky cat lovers to the Catsbury Park coffee shop. Rainbow flags welcome LGBTQ visitors and allies.

And yet while tattoos and beards and gays and dog and cat lovers are welcome and encouraged, not all kinds of diversity are accepted in Asbury Park. As a Haitian American interviewee explains, "Any place that plays Black music, we close them down. No Black-owned liquor licenses in Asbury. Nowhere that exclusively plays hip-hop. No liquor licenses on [the] west side of town. Dress codes—no plain white T-shirts, no Timbs, no baseball caps."[12] She says of new residents, "They move next to the high school and then complain about kids walking down the street. Kids had a balloon fight, and people called them 'animals' and 'savages' and asked for extra police protections. They are mostly White middle-class folks. I see their pictures." We heard more than once about discriminatory policies regarding what type of music can be featured in the venues of Asbury Park. Some forms of diversity are clearly valued above others. Antonia Randolph, in her book *The Wrong Kind of Different*, writes about how classroom teachers have a hierarchy of diversity and favor some students, such as certain immigrant minorities, over others, such as low-income Black students.[13] These same preferences can be seen in urban redevelopment; for example, Florida uses a "Gay Index" to determine tolerance and the creative acceptance of a city, not demographic numbers, which would show communities with large proportions of Black residents, thus his index privileges certain types of diversity over others.

So will the diversity in Asbury Park be maintained? And if so, how? Will longtime residents sell? One of our Haitian American interviewees explains, "Our home on the East Side. . . . Someone is always knocking on their door. People are coming and asking all the time. We love where we live, and we know the significance of land ownership and what it means for Haitians and African Americans to own land. We're not as tempted by the dollars. Unless you show up with forty acres and a mule, otherwise 'No, no, no'—it's not even half an acre." An LGBTQ activist notes his concerns over the loss of his community to gentrification: "I would cry the day I walk throughout this city and I can't find one rainbow flag." Another participant tells us about the seasonal gentrifiers who have already come to town and changed the ambiance: "Friday or Saturday night, those people are from NYC and Deal—there are Maseratis and BMWs. These people are already here."

Taming an Unruly Teenager: What Is Not Wanted in Asbury Park

Those who care deeply about the community do not want to see the boardwalk turned into a shopping mall, the waterfront become dotted with luxury high-rises or private beach clubs, or the community taken over by drunken shore tourists. As one small business owner pleads, "You know, obviously my fear of moving here is like—there's something really special. Please, please, please don't put high-rise buildings on the waterfront."

The question on people's minds is, Will the community flip and become made up of people who are not interested in community? One local states, "I think that's the biggest other threat that's going on—that sense of community is being challenged by people that just don't care. Like, 'Oh, I'm gonna make money off that, and I'm gonna be out. There's gonna be another place I can flip a house and then I'm gonna be out.' Whereas for a long time, it seemed like everybody sort of unified in a vision of 'I just want to live and work here.'" When corporatized gentrification or supergentrification occurs in communities, there is a known shift from residents who are less community minded to those who are investment minded and more insular.[14] One LGBTQ resident fears a shift such as this in Asbury: "I don't think they have the commitment to the city. [They're like,] 'I'm going to come and quickly make it not that much fun. I'm going to complain when there is music at Stone Pony or by bars.' We were at every board meeting for decades."

One small business owner explains a shift she has seen: "The East Side, which is, you know, you say it's just a bunch of drunk kids, but last night . . . somebody stole all the plants in front of Cardinal. Someone smashed a hole in the optometrist window, you know . . . and I'm like, 'This didn't happen ten years ago.' So I think the crystal ball right now is like, if I could compare it to anything, it's like having a really unruly sixteen-year-old who doesn't know who it is . . . and is really wooed by the flashy, bad kids."

An activist details his concerns over an important piece of property on the West Side: "So it represents both the history of the avenue when it was a regional destination point, and it represents the history of the avenue post–1970 riots. But it also represents the potential of the avenue . . . and the question is, How will that potential be fulfilled? Is it going to be a for-profit developer that wants the community out—doesn't care about community? Just wants to meet their margins and get out? Or does it represent the opportunity for something that has a broader, higher purpose serving the community?" His partner continues, "Ten years ago, there was probably a higher probability of that."

With the opening of the gleaming, glossy Asbury Ocean Club in 2019, this building seems representative of a new and different possible future for Asbury Park. While it is geographically close to the Asbury Hotel, the Ocean Club is nothing like it. When the Asbury Hotel opened, it seemed to represent a new era and a trendy, wealthier period for Asbury Park. While the hotel boasts a funky gallery with $100 framed portraits of Bruce Springsteen and other music memorabilia on its property, a lobby open to the public with billiards and shelves of old records, and a rooftop bar called Salvation in homage to its history (the hotel opened in 2016 in the former Salvation Army building), the Ocean Club could be a world away with its minimalist furnishings, heavily secured entrances, and a pool terrace with a bar and grille touted on their website as a "private oasis." It will also house a recreational cooking school (*not* a school where local residents can learn to cook for employment) and a healthy food market on the property. While a weekend rate (a month out) at the Asbury Hotel for one seasonal gentrifier in August 2019 is available for $367.50, the Ocean Club rooms available are listed from $450 to $1,050 per night. The seventeen-story windowed Ocean Club glitters in the sun with the sand on one side, and on the other side, only a few blocks away are the railroad tracks dividing the community. This represents for many longtime residents the dynamics of the citadel and the inequitable city Marcuse warned of in his powerful 1997 article "The Enclave, the Citadel, and the Ghetto."[15]

Divisions in Cool: The Case of the Sculpture Garden and the Trees

What is seen as cool or an improvement on the East Side is not always what West Siders want, and even if and when it is, locals on the West Side do not want changes imposed on them by "outsiders." Addressing this tension will be central to the city's ability to move forward as a unified entity. Through our research, we learned of two examples that illustrate this tension. The first involves a local Asbury artist who wanted to open a gallery to all of the community. She offered to work with youth on the West Side. While some suggested she do a mural with youth on the West Side, she felt that that would be basically "paint by numbers and no fun." She wanted to create a sculpture garden out of recycled materials instead, but that suggestion was met with resistance from West Siders who thought she wanted to put trash into their community. In her own defense, she sighted a similar project in Detroit. To us, she explains, "It's sad that they see garbage and I see sculptures. . . . I can't change that. I can bring them here and I can say that if I were a kid, I'd much rather learn how to make a sculpture than paint on a wall. I [also] wanted to do something with abandoned homes, but they said I needed West Side buy-in." The difference between her ideas and the Heidelberg Project in Detroit (which was not without pushback and has been somewhat destroyed by the city) is that Tyree Guyton, the artist behind the sculpture project in Detroit, was a Black man returning to Heidelberg, the street where he grew up, and using his art to make a statement. The project has indeed been very successful, and according to its website, "Residents who would never visit the Detroit Institute of Arts or the Detroit Symphony Orchestra have become educated about art and participate in HP programs, festivals and forums."[16] Bridging the divide between an East Side White woman and the West Side of Asbury, however, is a different project altogether.

The second example involves a street tree–planting initiative. Some Asbury Park residents who were part of the initiative had access to trees and decided to plant some of them on the West Side as part of a local move to better Asbury. However, longtime residents were not given buy-in, and when the West Siders saw the trees, they were angry, viewing this as the LGBTQ community coming in and disrupting their neighborhood. This was perceived as a kind of invasion. It was said that West Side residents then chopped down the trees.

The changing nature of the East Side, along with the inevitable tensions that arise when that coolness or the purveyors of that coolness on the East Side hit the West Side, raise significant concerns for Asbury Park's future. In addition, many of the early gentrifiers wonder if Asbury Park can maintain its current coolness or if the seasonal gentrification will progress to supergentrification— leaving behind even the current East Side residents and small businesses. If this happens, what are the implications of this for West Side residents, many of whom are already excluded?

As Asbury evolves, it will be essential to find a common ground uniting Asbury's East and West Side residents in resisting a future where both groups are marginalized—perhaps one that can provide economic opportunity for all residents and include full discussions about past and present racial inequality in the city and the potential effects of seasonal gentrification. Or will structural racism, the hot real estate market, and a history of inequality be barriers that are too great to overcome?

7

Land of Hope and Dreams?

During the 2019 Fourth of July celebrations in Asbury Park (forty-nine years to the day after the 1970 disturbances began), the sociological fault lines in the city seemed to us to symbolically crack wide open. The controversial Asbury Ocean Club, a glitzy hotel resort with high-end residences, had opened its doors on the boardwalk that weekend. This iStar mixed-use property, which boasts condominium prices ranging from $897,000 for a one-bedroom unit to $5.98 million for the penthouse, is a beautiful high-rise where glass windows abound, providing views of all of Asbury Park.[1] That weekend, the hotel guests, paying anywhere from $450 to a whopping $1,050 a night to stay in the rooftop penthouse, were privy to amenities characteristic of five-star Manhattan hotels. As the hotel guests might have been watching the Asbury Park firework display over the Atlantic Ocean, gunshots rang out on the boardwalk. Two women were injured, and a sixteen-year-old boy was arrested.[2] The gunshots, unsurprisingly, led to a panic, with tourists, workers, and residents all running for their lives.[3] In the shadow of the most expensive building on the boardwalk, and on the biggest night of the summer tourism season, the violence that we heard so much about but that was often confined to the city's West Side was visible for all to see.

The mayor, John Moor, was quick to respond publicly to the shooting, telling the local *Asbury Park Sun* newspaper, "What a terrible end to a beautiful day. We had a record-breaking turnout, what a shame it was a beautiful night." The mayor also lamented the presence of guns in Asbury and throughout the country to reporters: "My opinion, not the City's, there are just too many guns on the streets of all cities coming up legally or illegally from southern states."[4] A few weeks later, the city of Asbury Park presented five young White women who work at the Crepe Shop on the boardwalk with a proclamation honoring their bravery and assistance after the shooting. As the mayor and council were dealing with the aftermath of the July 4 shooting, just a few weeks later, on July 24, the town was rocked with a fatal police shooting of a civilian on the East Side two blocks from the boardwalk, and then just a few hours after that, police officers were called to a residence on the East Side, where one person was shot multiple times in the back.[5]

At the end of our writing, this appears to be where Asbury is situated. The city has gained press attention throughout the country and is often referred to as one of the "coolest" beach destinations. White middle-class young adults come to Asbury seeking work in the establishments of a gentrified city. The narrative that Asbury is a welcoming community can be evidenced on the boardwalk as rainbow flags fly high and "Hate Has No Home Here" signs hang in home and store windows. Vacationers flock to the beaches, restaurants, and bars; Bruce Springsteen makes surprise appearances on the Stone Pony Summer Stage; and the convention hall hosts events as diverse as mermaid parades and Christmas tree lightings. In many ways, Asbury Park has found its place, progressing beyond Frank Sinatra's infamous line, "Is it Granada I see, or only Asbury Park?"

Yet concerns abound as Asbury supporters grapple with the fallout of seasonal gentrification. The first round of gentrifiers now fear that the development is starting to push them out of town with high rents and climbing home prices. These fears are grounded in reality. Our analysis of Zillow data reveals that median home value among the top one-third of home values in the city increased 493 percent between April 1996 and March 2019, from $109,400 to $648,700.[6] In 1996, Asbury Park's top-tier home median value was ranked 504th among the states' towns and cities—within the lowest 10 percent. By 2019, the city's top-tier home median value was ranked 128th, within the top 25 percent. This was the greatest change in rank of any New Jersey locale. Among the ten cities experiencing the greatest changes in home value rank, four are Monmouth County towns near Asbury Park.[7]

And it is not just housing costs that concern residents. The LGBTQ community, who were instrumental in Asbury's revitalization in the 2000s and are often blamed for this gentrification, worry that the increasing costs may mean not only that home prices may become too high but that LGBTQ residents (particularly those of color) connected to the community could be displaced. Thus the inclusive, welcoming feel of the city may also change as the demographics shift.

Small business owners—many of whom believe in social justice—find themselves caught between their progressive ideals and their need to keep their businesses afloat. In most cases, the owners we met genuinely feel conflicted as they serve their predominately middle-class and White clientele, while just over the railroad tracks, longtime residents of color struggle to make ends meet. At the same time, they too raise concerns about the city's growth over the past years, fearful that they may no longer be able to run their businesses in town. In fact, in 2018, the boardwalk's only Black-owned business, the Asbury Galleria, was slated to close when the developer, Madison Marquette, did not renew the business's lease. At the time, Councilwoman Yvonne Clayton told the local paper, "I am very upset that the one African American owned business on the boardwalk is being forced to close. Kay has been there during the bad times and the good times, and this is how she is being paid back for her contribution to the city."[8] In addition to fears of displacement, several small business owners' situations are further compounded by seasonal gentrification—after the summer tourist season, how can they maintain their customer base and pay their rents?

As the East Side starts to grapple with the implications of seasonal gentrification, the longtime West Side residents continue to try to survive in an increasingly higher-income city. There are

TABLE 1. Ranked increase in New Jersey city
top-tier home prices, 1996–2019

CITY	MEDIAN HOME VALUE, APRIL 1996 ($)	MEDIAN HOME VALUE, MARCH 2019 ($)	MEDIAN HOME VALUE RANKING, APRIL 1996	MEDIAN HOME VALUE RANKING, MARCH 2019	RANKED CHANGE IN MEDIAN HOME VALUE RANKING, APRIL 1996–MARCH 2019
Asbury Park*	109,400	648,700	504	128	2
Bradley Beach*	152,800	873,300	384	73	3
Jersey City	149,700	799,800	390	83	4
North Wildwood	109,500	489,900	503	224	5
Lake Como*	134,200	578,400	443	164	6
West New York	142,900	580,700	414	162	7
Belmar*	185,600	956,600	301	56	8
Union City	141,100	563,600	420	179	9
West Cape May	172,600	702,300	342	113	10
Neptune*	138,000	459,200	430	246	10

SOURCE: Zillow Group Inc., Zillow Home Value Index.

NOTE: Home values are median values among the top one-third of local home values. Ranked change in median home value ranking compares cities' top-tier home price statewide rankings in April 1996 and March 2019.

* Indicates city in Monmouth County near or adjacent to Asbury Park.

some positive changes on the West Side. The job-training programs, such as the Kula Café and the Salt School, provide access to employment for some residents—many of whom fit the aesthetic labor—on the East Side. In addition, the revamped Springwood Park serves as a community hub on the West Side, bringing music into the air on warm summer nights and symbolizing some commitment to the West Side. However, Asbury remains the poorest city in the county, with a hypersegregated school system that is perceived by many as subpar, and too many residents, like Elijah's family, struggle to put food on the table and pay their bills. Moreover, racial tensions are very much at the center of the lives of West Side residents of color, as they live within a city and labor market that is embedded with racial inequality, adding structural barriers that compound their lives.

Present-day Asbury Park represents the nexus of seasonal gentrification, jobs, and race relations. However, the forces of seasonal gentrification create additional challenges that other gentrifying cities may not experience, much of which is further informed by Asbury's intersectionality. Since many of the new gentrifiers are second-home homeowners and not full-time residents, diversifying the school system seems less likely to occur. The school system also is not the highest priority for these newer residents and the companies and developers looking to please them and court more newcomers like them. And while job-training programs can connect some residents to employment opportunities, with a service economy that is dependent on summer tourism, those jobs may disappear as frost starts to line the store windows. Even if these positions last, only a few of the jobs lead to economic security. New Jersey's minimum wage law does not apply to tipped workers, meaning the base wage of the bartenders and waiters and waitresses in Asbury is just $2.13 an hour. Depending on a tipping structure is a precarious way to pay one's rent or put food on the table. The kinds of establishments opening are not particularly hiring-friendly to residents with criminal records but are also not amenities designed to serve and meet the needs of residents who live in Asbury year-round. The way forward for the city, then, must take into account not only the experience of gentrification and the lessons learned elsewhere but also the ways that seasonal gentrification compounds these issues.

We started our journey posing the question, What access do West Side residents have to the jobs that are being created on the East Side because of the gentrification of Asbury Park? Like so many projects, this question led to larger discussions about policing, education, access to amenities, housing, development, and the commodification of cool and then to our focus on seasonal gentrification and intersectionality. Thus our findings are mixed. In many ways, the existing job-training programs provide access to entry-level work, professional skills, and access to networks for some of the young residents of color. This is commendable and can lead to employment paths that can help those young people more toward more economically secure futures. Continuing to invest in these partnerships can help provide skills training and jobs to local residents. Concerns about the commodification of young people in Asbury certainly need to be part of the discussion to ensure that the young people are not just the brand being sold but truly part of the opportunity being afforded.

However, the opportunities for older West Side residents on the growing East Side seem less plentiful. Whether it is a lack of formal education, a criminal record, or just a poor fit on the East Side, many of these residents are being left behind. And when jobs are not plentiful for individuals in the private sector, it is sometimes necessary for the public sector to mandate the training and hiring. The building of high-rises, funded in part by public dollars, can require set-asides for local labor to ensure access to those construction jobs. However, our focus group members shared that they were not often included in those jobs. In many ways, the older residents were less hopeful about their futures in Asbury, and this group must be a focus of public-sector initiatives.

During our conversations with small business owners on the East Side, they shared a seemingly genuine desire to be good employers and community members. Yet whether it was the lack of resources to navigate a workforce development system, the lack of space and time to engage in outreach to West Side residents while trying to keep a business afloat in a seasonally gentrifying context, or the racial literacy needed to better engage the community, they often fell short of these hiring goals. City officials were seemingly eager to identify an economic policy that can democratize opportunity throughout the city. Training programs for employers in Asbury regarding inclusive hiring and antiracism and programs specifically geared toward older residents and ex-offenders could help strengthen and stabilize small businesses so they have the bandwidth to do this work well.

As evidenced in our work, challenges very much exist. Whether they involve some of the missteps that employers or even town officials make as they try to engage all Asbury Park residents or the lack of information on the West Side about programs that exist, there is no shortage of obstacles. Far too many of the West Side residents are unaware of free summer camps for their children or programs to secure free beach badges. And many potential workers with criminal records do not know about the bonding program as a potential route to employment. Town officials and other community leaders are learning that traditional communication channels (such as Nixle or social media) are not working. As one activist tells us, "I think one of the things that we learned [is] that the formal network of communications is more effective than any normal standard media. I think my conclusion is that folks in the area tend to distrust media, [the] tool we use for gathering data. Therefore, all the friends, cousin[s], [and] associates are much more effective." Thus these networks need to be mobilized to help undermine disinformation and share information about programs and job opportunities. Small business owners and gentrifiers also lack information on the true lived experiences of their West Side neighbors. And the initiatives that appear to be the most successful—such as Music Mondays in Springwood Park—sometimes only achieve success once they incorporate a lens of racial literacy. The same could be said of those that cite a lack of parent participation in the school as a barrier: the role of parents, the way parent involvement is defined, and the methods of reaching out may need to be reimagined.

Taking the lessons they have learned over the years, in 2016, the city received funding from the U.S. Department of Housing and Urban Development to develop a Choice Neighborhoods Plan to revitalize Asbury's West Side with housing, economic development, beautification projects, and educational opportunities. The plan was informed by residents throughout the city committed to improving opportunities to live and work. And in 2018, Wells Fargo made a $500,000 donation to Interfaith Neighbors to support projects in the town, such as affordable housing, economic development, employment, recreational programs, and family and community life.[9]

Work like that proposed in the Choice Neighborhoods Plan and these other local initiatives are promising and can help bridge some of the divides in town by investing in the West Side in ways that do not displace longtime residents. The Interfaith Neighbors is creating opportunities to purchase homes—a lot of them on the West Side. People we spoke with feel optimistic that this is what the residents have been waiting for and that it might also hopefully create a mixed-income community (with firefighters, school teachers, and people from the East Side) on the West Side. Residents understand the importance of bringing their voices to the table. As one West Side resident tells us, "And now we're at the point where we want change. So instead of looking at us— for lack of a better word—as bad, just like they weed out other people like they weed us out, then fine, but sit down and give some of us a chance to make difference, you know?"

The idea of an integrated town is, of course, appealing to locals. A more diverse downtown would bring the community together, which is something many residents miss about their hometown: "I loved that part of AP where people mingled, met, and shopped together. We have Super Extra store, [but] we need a good grocery store." In many ways, city officials and activists are trying to bring the two sides of Asbury together. Yet as scholar Derek Hyra argues, diversity itself is not enough. The diversity in the city is not benefiting the long-term residents, as civic groups such as churches, restaurants, recreation centers, and so on are still segregated. Instead, opportunities for meaningful interactions are critical to addressing structural poverty.[10]

Hyra goes on to note that affordable housing is critical, but it is not enough. Instead, he advocates for what he calls "neutral third spaces." In an interview with Tanvi Misra of CityLab, he says, "Public policy isn't geared toward funding community based organizations in gentrified areas that are trying to bring people together to dialogue about inequality or differences. It's not going to happen organically. There are very few foundations, a few city governments using their Community Development Block Grant (CDBG) money to focus on bridge-building. I really think we need that. We need affordable housing first, but we have to go beyond housing to make mixed-income, mixed-race communities work for everybody—to make them more inclusive."[11]

Hyra recommends ensuring the long-term existence of not only low-income residents but also small businesses to maintain that inclusiveness. The new progressive housing legislation of the city and plans like One Asbury are attempting to do this, but they still exist in the shadows of multi-million-dollar housing that is being constructed. Can these coexist? The concern growing in Asbury is that they cannot. The Save The North Beach community group remains active against iStar's plans to develop the north end of the beach, representing community activists, residents, and small business owners. And as one tourist says, "But now we are a little fearful of what is coming—who can afford the rents, and you might see chains coming in. See what's happened on Washington Street in Hoboken, and all the mom-and-pop [stores] are gone. I'm perfectly guilty of wanting to go into these places easily, but if you see those mall-type surf shops in Asbury, do I want to see that? No! My husband, he'll yell, 'This is just like Hoboken!'"

In some ways, trying to bring the city together into One Asbury forces the town leaders and residents to uncover some hard truths and grapple with intersecting systems of inequality. As one activist tells us,

> Asbury is a microcosm to me of any other small city in America because I come from Bed-Stuy, Brooklyn, and now it's full of—gentrified like crazy over in the last, say, five years. I've been out of New York seven years, and it's like you wouldn't know it. So Asbury is a small microcosm of what's going on . . . like people have said unless we address the economics . . . the racist discrimination that goes on in this country overall. But every politician comes in with a promise that doesn't mean anything, and like I said, jobs by itself doesn't mean anything too unless you have

economic development. So I think the conversation should really go to another level about inclusiveness.

One small business owner shares that they would like to have the future Asbury "have some cracked sidewalks." They continue, "I would like renewal of what's existing, and I would really love to see the disenfranchised know that they can participate in a meaningful way, and I can't speak to their home life, which I'm sure is challenging, but if our schools could actually support more of that, I think it could be—it could continue to be an oasis of multicultured, creative thought and community." And perhaps that is the advantage Asbury has: the dedicated networks of residents, business owners, and community leaders to better ensure that all voices can be heard to maintain what is authentically Asbury while also addressing the town's history of racism.

With the calls for the removal of the James A. Bradley statue, the structural racism that was embedded in the town founding could no longer be hidden. Having those conversations across the town, ensuring full representation of all residents in policy and programmatic planning, and working hard to evaluate policies with a racial lens can help build and strengthen those relationships.

Asbury, like many other cities faced with the realities of gentrification, must prioritize keeping and supporting housing for low-income and working-class residents. It is often the most at-risk residents who are the first to be displaced from a community when public housing is shuttered, converted, or privatized. Asbury must protect this population by enacting progressive policies that go beyond those required (as they are doing), creating community land trusts, supporting local organizations creating housing opportunities, and even looking abroad to approaches like the promising Vienna model.[12] Without maintaining the socioeconomic diversity of Asbury Park, all other efforts to maintain its character and spirit will be moot. Middle-income housing and opportunities to purchase must also be aggressively supported to protect the city from becoming one of only haves and have-nots. David

Price, executive director of Nuestra Comunidad Development Corporation, which serves Roxbury, Massachusetts, recommends additional protections in areas that are at risk of fully gentrifying that include tax protections for longtime residents, home repair funding for seniors, vouchers to stay in one's own community as it gentrifies (stabilization vouchers), and shifts to fair housing legislation.[13] Educating local residents and citizens about gentrification and giving them a seat at the table is also necessary. Attention must be paid to education reform policies, and these must protect against the further creation of a parallel education system for the children of those with means. In Asbury Park, those sixty-five and older represent approximately 11 percent of the population.[14] This is a population that is particularly susceptible to gentrification. Additionally, Asbury has an older housing stock, with 33.6 percent of residences built in 1939 or earlier, making them ripe for redevelopment or costly to maintain for property owners and those longtime residents trying to stay or keep their assets within the family.[15] Thus policies to protect seniors and longtime homeowners will prove valuable.

A key part of the real inclusiveness that can be maintained in Asbury if housing protections and opportunities for West Siders are put in place is helping facilitate access to the East Side amenities for West Side residents and improving the amenities on the West Side itself. A new e-scooter program began in August 2019, which could mitigate transportation barriers that West Side residents report. E-scooters and dockless bikes have been found to appeal to a different demographic than traditional bike-share programs and might be attractive to residents of color on the West Side.[16] However, this will not help families, seniors, or those with disabilities better access the beach. Avenues such as low-cost community shuttles or new parking policies could be explored.[17] Using existing community networks such as churches to spread information about employment, social programs, and city public events can help bring awareness of opportunities. It is important for those who want to disseminate guidance throughout the city to remember that different strategies will need to be implemented on the West Side.

In addition, city officials must find ways to ensure economic security for residents in the town. The jobs that are plentiful on the East Side tend to be lower-paying service-sector work. New Jersey did pass a minimum wage increase that will raise the minimum wage to $15 an hour by 2024, helping improve worker incomes in this industry. Yet as part of that law, seasonal workers and workers in small businesses (those with six or fewer employees) will see a slower increase, not earning $15 an hour until 2026. And tipped workers will stay in the $2 an hour range until 2020, when the tipped wage reaches $3.33 an hour, and then the rate will increase to $5.13 an hour by 2022. As the latter categories represent many of the jobs in Asbury, the road to economic security will be longer.[18] As such, it may be up to the city government to help improve the pay for these workers. Asbury Park officials should hold discussions with both workers and business owners to identify strategies to support both groups in helping workers reach living wages. In addition, in consultation with business owners and community groups, supporting leadership programs can help young people develop careers in hospitality and diversify the pipeline. The leadership program at the Salt School provides one model to build from.

City officials must continue to support private-public partnerships that promote local job training. The Kula Café and the Salt School, along with the Summer Youth Employment programs, for example, are effective in providing training, job experience, and professional skills. Working to expand the reach of these programs and engage more small business owners will help target training and increase job placements. Continuing to embed careers and workforce development in the school system's curriculum will help disseminate career awareness and provide networking opportunities for young people.

For many people, however, particularly those who are older, a variety of factors coalesce to make it difficult for them to access job opportunities in the East Side labor market. Asbury Park officials should work with the New Jersey Department of Labor and Workforce Development to develop training programs aimed at middle-aged and older workers. For instance, high school diploma recovery programs along with targeted training in growing health care industries can provide routes to economic security. And education on expungement and other programs that can mitigate the impact of criminal records is essential for employability. Transportation barriers to job opportunities outside of Asbury Park (and outside of the hospitality sector) need to be addressed as well.

Further, we must acknowledge that gentrification is, as Lindsey Miller writes, "just one symptom of a greater problem: a political and economic environment in which even well-paid workers spend over half of their salaries on rent, allows almost two-thirds of our country's workers to be paid unlivable wages, and does not guarantee, or even actively promote, access to necessities like healthcare or quality education."[19] And as income inequality widens, both in Asbury and nationally, more previously middle-class residents will find themselves with less savings and wealth than previous generations. Meanwhile, the most affluent may increasingly have the means to invest in second homes. Therefore, if government officials (at the city, state, and federal levels) start to effectively address these larger issues—much of which is out of Asbury's direct control—it will also have a positive impact on the city itself.

There has been no shortage of plans to improve Asbury Park and the West Side specifically. Paul McEvily of Interfaith Neighbors told a reporter of meeting with Hazel Samuels, Asbury's then director of community development, in the early 2000s. Samuels pleaded with McEvily not to be just another person coming in yet again and asking the community what they need. She then showed him seventeen West Side revitalization plans on the shelf that had never been implemented.[20] Our goal in this book is not to add another plan to the shelf but instead to tell the story of Asbury Park as it sits on a precipice and to tell it with an academic lens so that the experts—the community members—can have this information to assist them and so that researchers, academics, and community members elsewhere can learn from this city by the sea.

Seasonal gentrification is a new area of research, and we hope this study will lead to others that build and improve upon this one.

Asbury's story is still unfolding. As the town fights to save the North Beach from development and city officials try to better balance the incentives to developers with the changing realities of the city, this is coupled with a political moment in which issues of race, inclusiveness, and White privilege are increasingly part of the lexicon. The lessons from Asbury Park can help inform other places as they seasonally gentrify. As our ethnographic journey demonstrates, seasonal gentrification has lasting impacts. It is our hope that the people of Asbury have the momentum and support to create a more inclusive and equitable model city as opposed to just another "Brooklyn on the Beach."

Methodological Appendix

This book was a collaboration from the start. When we began working with one another at the City University of New York in 2015, we found that we both had an interest in Asbury Park, New Jersey, and that our individual research interests (Mary's in employment and workforce development and Molly's in gentrification and education) complemented our bubbling research questions about the community. The new hotels and restaurants in Asbury intrigued us both, and we were aware of the post-Fordist history of the community and curious if residents from socioeconomically disadvantaged backgrounds on the "other side of the tracks" were finding opportunities in these new venues.

To begin our data analysis, in 2015 we applied for a Professional Staff Congress (PSC) CUNY grant to begin asking these questions of the residents, employers, and activists in Asbury Park. We were awarded the grant, which then enabled us to hire two local research consultants—one a local activist to help us recruit participants and another a student to help us begin wrapping our head around the local context and media coverage. We also received funding for cash card stipends for focus group and interview participants. It was important to us to reach as deeply into Asbury's West Side as possible, and we felt a stipend would help us reach more residents.

As described in chapter 1, over the course of three years (2016–2019), we conducted in-depth interviews, held focus groups, and performed observational research in Asbury Park. Participants (N = 81) included eighteen community activists or educators involved in the West Side, thirty-four workers (or potential workers) from the West Side community, thirteen Asbury Park employers (including developers), four government representatives, three tourists / former residents, and nine seasonal employees working on the East Side. All the employers, save one, were White. Of the thirty-four workers from the West Side, only one identified as White-alone, and the rest identified as people of color. The community activists were half White and half individuals of color.

In the spring of 2017, we held a series of focus groups at a nonprofit center in Asbury Park on Springwood Avenue. One focus group was held with those who responded to our research assistant's recruitment of the activist network in Asbury Park. The purpose of this focus group was to understand how activists deeply engaged in the community see the gentrification and opportunities (or lack thereof) for the populations they work with and for. Mary and Molly cofacilitated that focus group. Another three focus groups were then conducted with those who identified as adult West Side residents. These were all residents of color, although that was not a requirement. Two focus groups had to be held simultaneously, each conducted by one of us in adjoining rooms, because so many community members came to participate. The purpose of these focus groups was to assess how West Side residents see the changes to Asbury Park, how they look for employment, what successes and challenges they have in finding employment, and their engagement with the East Side of Asbury. These participants were recruited through the activist network, the nonprofit center, and from our research consultant walking through the West Side community and literally asking people to come participate. Participants were given a $20 TD Bank cash card for participating. After this, Mary facilitated a focus group for community leaders at a local coffee shop. The purpose of this focus group was to better understand how leaders were experiencing and understanding the gentrification in the city and to provide them an avenue to share their perspectives and the work being accomplished. All focus groups were recorded and transcribed. We then interviewed thirteen employers from local small businesses and school advocates. We hoped to understand what challenges and successes local employers had experienced in hiring locally and how students in Asbury were connected with employers and work. These semistructured in-person interviews were largely conducted in their places of business, some were cofacilitated, and some were conducted by Mary alone.

At that juncture, we began to see areas of the story that were not as well represented, so we worked to plan a Latinx focus group. Recruiting for this proved a challenge (perhaps in part because stories and fears about ICE were high in 2017). We did not want to do any visible recruitment that could make potential participants nervous. After reaching out to different community members, we were able to schedule a focus group at another local nonprofit center. We cofacilitated this focus group, provided a translator, and participants received a $20 TD Bank cash card. This focus group was entirely women, although this was not on purpose. At this point, we wanted to further understand what we had heard and to tell stories emerging in our data collection (like the history of the LGBTQ community in Asbury Park) that we realized during our research were largely untold. We then interviewed additional middle-class residents, LGBTQ activists, and tourists and met with politicians and developers to understand the full story. These interviews and discussions took place on both the East and West Sides and outside of Asbury in northern New Jersey in places such as coffee shops, restaurants, and offices from 2016 to 2019. We also wanted to tell a more in-depth story, which is how we ended up sitting with Elijah (a pseudonym) at a local nonprofit that had assisted us. We paid Elijah a cash incentive to do the interview (which, as we explain in chapter 5, he gave away in front of us). All interviews were transcribed. After we had completed all data collection, the transcriptions were double coded.

In our qualitative data collection, we tried to keep the interaction as natural as possible. We typically began by explaining the project, sharing our experiences living in New Jersey, and discussing our past research interests. This helped break the ice at the beginning of the interview and increased the comfort level of our conversation. We also encouraged participants to reach out if they had additional thoughts after our discussions. Some did send us follow-up thoughts or related articles or questions. We are aware that we are two White middle-class professors who do not live in Asbury Park. And despite our efforts to make participants feel comfortable, we were "outsiders" to many of our interviewees. It is then impossible to ever fully know how our presence influenced our data collection and how our positionality impacted our work. It is our hope that the experiences of the Asbury Park residents, visitors, and small business owners shared in this book will inform intersectional thinking and antiracist policies in the city and be a model for other cities.

In addition to interviews and focus groups, we spent countless hours participating in ethnographic observations of Asbury Park life. We ate at restaurants, stayed at hotels, listened to music at concerts, attended conventions and festivals and rallies, sunbathed at the beaches, attended meetings of city government, and walked throughout the East and West Sides. We had many formal and informal conversations with city officials, residents, workers, and tourists.

As this book was coming together, we applied for a second PSC-CUNY grant, which we received. This grant enabled us to hire a research consultant, Shawn McMahon, to analyze U.S. Census Bureau, U.S. Consumer Financial Protection Bureau, and Zillow Group Inc. data. After completing our initial analysis, we evaluated the work of Alicia Raia-Hawrylak on children and their parents in Asbury Park and the article "Revitalization Greetings from Asbury Park" by Chris Pomorski, which both supported our conclusions.[1]

No names are used in the book except for those of public figures who spoke to us in their professional capacity and were given the opportunity to look at quotes in advance of publication. We grouped individuals into categories such as "activist," "small business owner," "developer," and "tourist" to help protect the individual identities of those who participated in our work. When necessary for understanding the findings, participants may be identified by more specific descriptors, such as "LGBTQ" or by their race, ethnicity, or gender. All these individuals we encountered believed in Asbury Park and were willing to give their time and attention to this cause.

Out of the data collection came this story of seasonality and gentrification and the deep intersectionalities at play in the community. Our initial theme of employment then led to the themes in chapters 5 and 6: beach/boardwalk access, policing, education, supports for children/families, and the commodification of cool. By engaging in a multiyear ethnographic journey in Asbury Park, we were able to go beyond the beach to share the stories of residents, workers, tourists, employers, and city leaders. It is our hope that our methods did justice to their lived experiences.

Acknowledgments

This book would not have been possible without the support of numerous individuals. We had the great pleasure of working with many Asbury Park residents over the years who are, of course, the true experts on this topic.

We would also like to thank the following people who assisted with our work: our quantitative data consultant, Shawn McMahon, who analyzed a significant amount of data to frame our ethnography and went above and beyond by looking over and improving the manuscript in its entirety; our Asbury Park qualitative research consultant, Randy Thompson (founder of Help Not Handcuffs), who helped us in our outreach for interviews and focus groups; Christie Rhodes, who assisted with our initial research; and our photographer, Erika Bentley Leonard, whose photographs help bring our book to life.

We appreciate the creativity and expertise of our students Marcos Montesinos and Jalen Bridges and the insights from our colleague Marcus Allen and our friends Chris Chambers, Ramona Chambers, Dorothy Knauer, Sandy Lizaire-Duff, Cara Kronen, Te-Sheng (Emery) Huang, Ryan Coughlan, and Darby Corna Vinciguerra as we brainstormed titles and ideas. Thank you to the organizations and people who provided spaces for us to conduct our work and helped us with outreach. We are grateful for the grant funding from the Professional Staff Congress CUNY, which allowed us to complete the ethnographic and quantitative research. We also thank Peter Mickulas, our editor at Rutgers Press, who was excited about this book from the very start and saw its promise in its earliest stages.

Finally, we are grateful to our partners, Jeff Makris and Mike Glory, who graciously provided us the space and time to undertake an ethnographic investigation. Everyone who touched this book made it better, but all mistakes are all our own.

Notes

1. Seasonal Gentrification

1. Chris Pomorski, "Revitalization Greetings from Asbury Park," *Next City*, August 15, 2016, https://nextcity.org/features/view/new-jersey-asbury -park-redevelopment.

2. David Goldberg, *The Retreats of Reconstruction* (New York: Fordham University Press, 2017).

3. Japonica Brown-Saracino, *The Gentrification Debates* (New York: Routledge, 2010), 13.

4. Gina Perez, *The Near Northwest Side Story: Migration, Displacement, and Puerto Rican Families* (Berkeley: University of California Press, 2004), 139.

5. Robert Firpo-Cappiellois, "Meet the Coolest Small Town in America," Budget Travel, June 2, 2017, https://www.budgettravel.com/article/meet -the-coolest-small-town-in-america-2017.

6. U.S. Census Bureau, *2006–2010 American Community Survey 5-Year Estimates, Table S1501*, generated by Shawn McMahon using American FactFinder, accessed July 2, 2019, http://factfinder.census.gov; U.S. Census Bureau, *2013–2017 American Community Survey 5-Year Estimates, Table S1501*, generated by Shawn McMahon using American FactFinder, accessed July 2, 2019, https://factfinder.census.gov.

7. U.S. Census Bureau, *2008–2012 American Community Survey 5-Year Estimates, Table CP03*, generated by Shawn McMahon using American FactFinder, accessed July 27, 2019, https://factfinder.census.gov; U.S. Census Bureau, *2013–2017 American Community Survey 5-Year Estimates, Table CP03*, generated by Shawn McMahon using American FactFinder, accessed July 27, 2019, http://factfinder.census.gov.

8. U.S. Census Bureau, *2013–2017 American Community Survey 5-Year Estimates, Table S1901*, generated by Shawn McMahon using American FactFinder, accessed August 28, 2019, https://factfinder.census.gov; Federal Housing Finance Agency, "National Mortgage Database," accessed June 22, 2019, https://www.fhfa.gov/PolicyProgramsResearch/Programs/Pages/National-Mortgage-Database.aspx; U.S. Census Bureau, *2013–2017 American Community Survey 5-Year Estimates, Table DP04*, generated by Shawn McMahon, using American FactFinder, accessed July 17, 2019, https://factfinder.census.gov.

9. U.S. Census Bureau, *2008–2012 American Community Survey 5-Year Estimates, Table DP04*, generated by Shawn McMahon, using American FactFinder, accessed July 17, 2019, https://factfinder.census.gov; U.S. Census Bureau, *2013–2017, Table DP04*.

10. Federal Housing Finance Agency, "National Mortgage Database."

11. U.S. Census Bureau, *2006–2010 American Community Survey 5-Year Estimates, Table C15002*, generated by Shawn McMahon, using American FactFinder, accessed July 2, 2019, https://factfinder.census.gov; U.S. Census Bureau, *2013–2017 American Community Survey 5-Year Estimates, Table C15002*, generated by Shawn McMahon, using American FactFinder, accessed July 2, 2019, https://factfinder.census.gov.

12. U.S. Census Bureau, *Census 2000 Summary File 1, Table DP-1*, generated by Shawn McMahon, using American FactFinder, accessed July 16, 2019, https://factfinder.census.gov; U.S. Census Bureau, *2013–2017 American Community Survey 5-Year Estimates, Table S0101*, generated by Shawn McMahon, using American FactFinder, accessed June 20, 2019, http://factfinder.census.gov.

13. U.S. Census Bureau, *2006–2010 American Community Survey 5-Year Estimates, Table S1701*, generated by Shawn McMahon, using American FactFinder, accessed July 16, 2019, https://factfinder.census.gov; U.S. Census Bureau, *2013–2017 American Community Survey 5-Year Estimates, Table S1701*, generated by Shawn McMahon, using American FactFinder, accessed July 16, 2019, https://factfinder.census.gov.

14. Due to small sample sizes, substantial potential margins of error accompany American Community Survey data on employment figures for smaller occupations and industries, local rents, income by family type, median income by race, and poverty rates and educational attainment by

race. Housing data herein is drawn from the U.S. Consumer Financial Protection Bureau's Home Mortgage Disclosure Act Database and from Zillow.com and are population data; margins of error are therefore not of concern as they are with American Community Survey data. Education data are drawn from NJ School Performance Reports and represent Asbury Park's school population.

15. Austin Bogues and Ryan Ross, "Asbury Park Ranked among 50 Worst United States Cities to Live In," *Asbury Park Press*, February 7, 2019, https://www.app.com/story/news/local/how-we-live/2019/02/07/asbury -park-worst-united-states-cities/2800228002/.

16. Save Asbury's Waterfront is a collaborative effort of community leaders, residents, and business owners who have come together to organize against the iStar development of the north end of the Asbury beachfront. For more information, see https://saveasburypark.surfrider.org/.

17. Austin Bogues, "Esperanza Site Renamed Asbury Ocean Club Surfside Resort and Residences," *Asbury Park Press*, May 9, 2018, https://www .app.com/story/news/local/communitychange/2018/05/09/asbury-park -esperanza-site-renamed-asbury-ocean-club/592837002/.

18. Asbury Ocean Club, "Asbury Ocean Club Amenities," accessed August 2019, https://asburyoceanclub.com/amenities/.

19. Steve Strunsky, "Asbury Park Says Aggressive Panhandling Is 'Embarrassing,' So the City Banned It," NJ.com, October 29, 2018, https://www .nj.com/monmouth/2018/10/asbury_park_bans_aggressive_panhandling .html.

20. Austin Bogues, "Asbury Park Bans Smoking at the Beaches," *Asbury Park Press*, April 27, 2018, https://www.app.com/story/news/local/ communitychange/2018/04/27/asbury-park-bans-smoking-beaches/ 557837002/.

21. U.S. Consumer Financial Protection Bureau, Home Mortgage Disclosure Act Database, accessed July 18, 2019, https://www.consumerfinance .gov/data-research/hmda/.

22. U.S. Consumer Financial Protection Bureau.

23. U.S. Census Bureau, *2013–2017 American Community Survey 5-Year Estimates, Table B25003*, generated by Shawn McMahon, using American FactFinder, accessed August 28, 2019, https://factfinder.census .gov.

24. "Asbury Park's Progressive Approach to Tackle a Major Issue," *triCityNews*, March 21, 2019, 24, 59.

25. These are redevelopment areas on the West Side.

26. APAHC, quoted in "Asbury Park's Progressive Approach," 59.

27. "Asbury Park Likely Buying Beach Property to Stop iStar Development," *Real Deal*, March 12, 2009, https://therealdeal.com/2019/03/12/asbury-park-looks-at-buying-beach-property-to-stop-istar-development/.

28. John Joe Schlichtman, Jason Patch, and Marc Lamont Hill, *Gentrifier* (Toronto: University of Toronto Press, 2017), 9.

29. Brian J. Berry, "Islands of Renewal in Seas of Decay," in *The New Urban Reality*, by Brian J. Berry, ed. Paul E. Peterson (Washington, D.C.: Brookings Institute, 1985), 69–96; Lois Willie, *At Home in the Loop: How Clout and Community Built Chicago's Dearborn Park* (Carbondale: Southern Illinois University Press, 1998); Jacob L. Vigdor, Douglas S. Massey, and Alice Rivlin, "Does Gentrification Harm the Poor?," *Brookings-Wharton Papers on Urban Affairs* (2002): 133–182, https://www.jstor.org/stable/25067387; Richard L. Florida, *The Rise of the Creative Class: And How It's Transforming Work, Leisure, Community and Everyday Life* (New York: Basic Books, 2002); Richard Florida, "Cities and the Creative Class," *City and Community* 2, no. 1 (2003): 3–18, https://doi.org/10.1111/1540-6040.00034; Lance Freeman, *There Goes the "Hood": Views of Gentrification from the Ground Up* (Philadelphia: Temple University Press, 2006); Rachel Meltzer and Jenny Schuetz, "Bodegas or Bagel Shops? Neighborhood Differences in Retail & Household Services," *Economic Development Quarterly* 26, no. 1 (2012): 73–94.

30. Peter Marcuse, "The Enclave, the Citadel, and the Ghetto: What Has Changed in the Post-Fordist U.S. City," *Urban Affairs Review* 33, no. 2 (1997): 228–264; Neil Smith, *The New Urban Frontier: Gentrification and the Revanchist City* (London: Routledge, 1996); Perez, *Near Northwest Side Story*; Mario Luis Small, *Villa Victoria: The Transformation of Social Capital in a Boston Barrio* (Chicago: University of Chicago Press, 2004); Kathe Newman and Elvin Wyly, "The Right to Stay Put, Revisited: Gentrification and Resistance to Displacement in New York City," *Urban Studies* 43, no. 1 (2006): 44–52, https://doi.org/10.1080/00420980500388710; Mary Patillo, *Black on the Block* (Chicago:

University of Chicago Press, 2008); Sharon Zukin, *Naked City: The Death and Life of Authentic Urban Places* (New York: Oxford University Press, 2009); Daniel Monroe Sullivan and Samuel Shaw, "Retail Gentrification and Race: The Case of Alberta Street in Portland, Oregon," *Urban Affairs Review* 47, no. 3 (2011): 413–432; L. Posey-Maddox, *When Middle-Class Parents Choose Urban Schools: Class, Race, and the Challenge of Equity in Public Education* (Chicago: University of Chicago Press, 2014); Molly Vollman Makris, *Public Housing and School Choice in a Gentrified City: Youth Experiences of Uneven Opportunity* (New York: Palgrave Macmillan, 2015).

31. Smith, *New Urban Frontier*; David Ley, *The New Middle Class and the Remaking of the Central City* (Oxford: Oxford University Press, 1996).

32. Laurence A. G. Moss, *The Amenity Migrants: Seeking and Sustaining Mountains and Their Cultures* (Oxfordshire, U.K.: CAB International North America, 2006); Eliza Darling, "The City in the Country: Wilderness Gentrification and the Rent Gap," *Environment and Planning A: Economy and Space* 37, no. 6 (2005): 1015–1032, https://doi.org/10.1068/a37158.

33. Manfred Perlik, "Alpine Gentrification: The Mountain Village as a Metropolitan Neighbourhood," *Journal of Alpine Research* 99 (2011), https://journals.openedition.org/rga/1370?gathStatIcon=true&lang=en.

34. Chris Paris, "Re-positioning Second Homes within Housing Studies: Household Investment, Gentrification, Multiple Residence, Mobility and Hyper-consumption," *Housing Theory and Society* 26, no. 4 (2009): 292.

35. David Hyra, *Race, Class, and Politics in the Cappuccino City* (Chicago: University of Chicago Press, 2017).

36. Troy McMullen, "Historically Black Beach Enclaves Are Fighting to Save Their History and Identity," *Washington Post*, July 7, 2017, https://www.washingtonpost.com/realestate/surf-sand-and-race/2017/07/26/f674c5be-61bb-11e7-84a1-a26b75ad39fe_story.html.

37. Saskia Sassen, *The Global City: New York, London, Tokyo* (Princeton, N.J.: Princeton University Press, 2001); Ley, *New Middle Class*.

38. Meltzer and Schuetz, "Bodegas or Bagel Shops?"; Jenny Schuetz, Jed Kolko, and Rachel Meltzer, "Are Poor Neighborhoods 'Retail Deserts'?," *Regional Science and Urban Economics* 42, nos. 1–2 (2012): 269–285,

https://doi.org/10.1016/j.regsciurbeco.2011.09.005; Karen Chapple and
Rick Jacobus, "Retail Trade as a Route to Neighborhood Revitalization,"
in *Urban and Regional Policy and Its Effects*, ed. Nancy Pindus, Howard
Wial, and Harold Wolman (Washington, D.C.: Brookings Institution
Press, 2009), http://www.jstor.org/stable/10.7864/j.ctt127zb9; Zukin,
Naked City.

39. Jed Kolko, "Job Location, Neighborhood Change, and Gentrification"
(working paper, Public Policy Institute of California, 2009), https://dx
.doi.org/10.2139/ssrn.1662548.

40. T. William Lester and Daniel Hartley, "The Long Term Employment
Impacts of Gentrification in the 1990s," *Regional Science and Urban
Economics* 45 (2014): 80–89; Winifred Curran, "Gentrification and the
Nature of Work: Exploring the Links in Williamsburg, Brooklyn,"
Environment and Planning 36 (2004): 1243–1258; Rachel Meltzer and
Pooya Ghorbani, "Does Gentrification Increase Employment Oppor-
tunities in Low-Income Neighborhoods?," *Regional Science and Urban
Economics* 66 (2017): 52–73.

41. Neil Argent, Matthew Tonts, Roy Jones, and John Holmes, "A
Creativity-Led Rural Renaissance? Amenity-Led Migration, the Cre-
ative Turn and the Uneven Development of Rural Australia," *Applied
Geography* 44 (2013): 88–98.

42. See our methodological appendix for greater details on our ethnographic
methods.

43. Alicia Raia-Hawrylak, "Youth Experiences of Space in a Gentrifying
Community: A Case Study of Asbury Park," in *Soul of Society: A Focus on
the Lives of Children & Youth*, ed. Mary Nicole Warehime (Bingley, U.K.:
Emerald Group, 2014); Chris Pomorski, "Revitalization Greetings from
Asbury Park," *Next City*, August 15, 2016, https://nextcity.org/features/
view/new-jersey-asbury-park-redevelopment.

2. Racial Segregation, Sex, Gender, and Rock 'n' Roll

1. C. Jordan, "Bruce Springsteen Dances with His Mom at Wonder Bar
to Celebrate Her Birthday," *Asbury Park Press*, April 15, 2018, https://
www.app.com/story/entertainment/music/2018/04/15/bruce-springsteen
-dances-mom-wonder-bar-celebrate-her-birthday/519361002/.

2. Kimberle Crenshaw, "Demarginalizing the Intersection of Race and Sex: A Black Feminist Critique of Antidiscrimination Doctrine, Feminist Theory and Antiracist Politics," *University of Chicago Legal Forum* 1989 (1989), https://chicagounbound.uchicago.edu/uclf/vol1989/iss1/8/.

3. Chris Pomorski, "Revitalization Greetings from Asbury Park," *Next City*, August 15, 2016, https://nextcity.org/features/view/new-jersey-asbury-park-redevelopment.

4. David Goldberg, "Greetings from Jim Crow, New Jersey: Contesting the Meaning and Abandonment of Reconstruction in the Public and Commercial Spaces of Asbury Park, 1880–1890," *Concept* 30 (2007), https://concept.journals.villanova.edu/article/view/279.

5. Chris Pomorski, "Revitalization Greetings from Asbury Park," *Next City*, August 15, 2016, https://nextcity.org/features/view/new-jersey-asbury-park-redevelopment.

6. Goldberg, "Greetings from Jim Crow."

7. Bryant Simon, *Boardwalk of Dreams: Atlantic City and the Fate of Urban America* (New York: Oxford University Press, 2006); Goldberg, "Greetings from Jim Crow."

8. Austin Bogues, "In 1968, Music Saved Asbury Park," *Asbury Park Press*, July 10, 2018, https://www.app.com/story/entertainment/2018/07/10/1968-music-saved-asbury-park/632729002/.

9. Katrina Martin, "The Asbury Park July 1970 Riots," *Devil's Tale* (blog), Duke University Libraries, June 28, 2016, https://blogs.library.duke.edu/rubenstein/2016/06/28/asbury-park-july-1970-riots/.

10. Charles Bagli, "Asbury Park Long Neglected Shows Signs of Rejuvenation," *New York Times*, August 1, 2015, https://www.nytimes.com/2015/08/01/nyregion/asbury-park-long-neglected-shows-signs-of-rejuvenation.html.

11. Bogues, "In 1968."

12. Jean Mikie, "U2 Played Twice at This Legendary Asbury Park Club," *Asbury Park Press*, November 9, 2014, https://www.app.com/story/news/local/eatontown-asbury-park/asbury-park/2014/11/09/u-played-twice-legendary-asbury-park-club/18756973/.

13. David Christafore and Susane Leguizamon, "Is 'Gaytrification' a Real Phenomenon?," *Urban Affairs Review* 54, no. 5 (2018), https://doi.org/10.1177/1078087416682321, abstract.

14. C. Jordan, "Judy Garland's Really Bad Week at the Jersey Shore," *Asbury Park Press*, June 26, 2018, https://www.app.com/story/entertainment/music/2018/06/26/judy-garlands-really-bad-week-jersey-shore-50th-year-anniversary/734441002/.

15. Tennyson Coleman, "How Asbury Park's Paradise Became One of the Oldest (but Still Hottest) Gay Club in N.J.," NJ.com, July 2, 2019, https://www.nj.com/entertainment/2019/06/heres-how-asbury-parks-paradise-became-the-oldest-but-still-hottest-gay-club-in-nj.html.

16. J. Thomas, "The Gay Bar: Why the Gay Rights Movement Was Born in One," Slate, June 28, 2011.

17. Coleman, "How Asbury Park's Paradise."

18. Jason Hackworth, "Postrecession Gentrification in New York City," *Urban Affairs Review* 37 (2002): 815–843, https://journals.sagepub.com/doi/10.1177/107874037006003.

19. Kathe Newman and Elvin Wyly, "The Right to Stay Put, Revisited: Gentrification and Resistance to Displacement in New York City," *Urban Studies* 43, no. 1 (2006): 45, https://doi.org/10.1080/00420980500388710.

20. Dan Jacobson, "Time to Honor Historic LGBT Moment in Asbury Park," *triCityNews*, August 22, 2019, 25.

21. Laura Durso and Gary Gates, *Serving Our Youth: Findings from a National Survey of Service Providers Working with Lesbian, Gay, Bisexual, and Transgender Youth Who Are Homeless or At Risk of Becoming Homeless* (Los Angeles: Williams Institute, 2012).

22. Amin Ghaziani, *There Goes the Gayborhood?* (Princeton, N.J.: Princeton University Press, 2014); Kath Weston, "Get Thee to a Big City: Sexual Imaginary and the Great Gay Migration," *GLQ* 2, no. 3 (1995): 253–277.

23. Ghaziani, *There Goes the Gayborhood?*

24. N. Terry, "Asbury's Political Power Struggle," *Asbury Park Press*, October 14, 2014, https://www.app.com/story/news/local/eatontown-asbury-park/asbury-park/2014/10/14/asbury-parks-power-struggle/17276145/.

25. Bagli, "Asbury Park Long Neglected."

26. U.S. Census Bureau, *2013–2017 American Community Survey 5-Year Estimates, Table S1701*, generated by Shawn McMahon, using American FactFinder, accessed July 16, 2019, https://factfinder.census.gov.

27. U.S. Census Bureau, *2013–2017 American Community Survey 5-Year Estimates, Table C15002*, generated by Shawn McMahon, using American FactFinder, accessed July 2, 2019, https://factfinder.census.gov.

28. U.S. Census Bureau, *2013–2017 American Community Survey 5-Year Estimates, Table B20017*, generated by Shawn McMahon, using American FactFinder, accessed August 28, 2019, http://factfinder.census.gov.

29. U.S. Census Bureau, *2013–2017 American Community Survey 5-Year Estimates, Table DP05*, generated by Shawn McMahon, using American FactFinder, accessed August 28, 2019, http://factfinder.census.gov.

30. U.S. Census Bureau, *2013–2017 American Community Survey 5-Year Estimates, Table B05002*, generated by Shawn McMahon, using American FactFinder, accessed August 28, 2019, http://factfinder.census.gov; U.S. Census Bureau, *2013–2017 American Community Survey 5-Year Estimates, Table S1601*, generated by Shawn McMahon, using American Fact-Finder, accessed August 28, 2019, http://factfinder.census.gov.

31. State of New Jersey Department of Education, *New Jersey School Performance Reports 2015–2016 & 2017–2018*, accessed September 2017 and August 1, 2019, https://rc.doe.state.nj.us/report.aspx?County=25& District=0100&School=010&SchoolYear=2015-2016&SY=1516.

32. Jessica Glenza, "New Jersey Town Made Famous by Springsteen at Centre of Gentrification Row," *Guardian*, June 17, 2018, https://www.theguardian .com/us-news/2018/jun/17/bruce-springsteen-asbury-park-new-jersey.

33. Jill P. Capuzzo, "Asbury Park's Long Recovery," *New York Times*, December 7, 2003, https://www.nytimes.com/2003/12/07/nyregion/asbury-park -s-long-recovery.html; Julie Besonen, "Asbury Park: Where Art, Grit, and Local Spirits Mix," *New York Times*, August 4, 2017, https://www .nytimes.com/2017/08/04/nyregion/asbury-park.html.

34. U.S. Census Bureau, *2006–2010 American Community Survey 5-Year Estimates, Table B25013*, generated by Shawn McMahon using American FactFinder, accessed August 28, 2019, http://factfinder.census.gov; U.S. Census Bureau, *2013–2017 American Community Survey 5-Year Estimates, Table B25013*, generated by Shawn McMahon using American Fact-Finder, accessed August 28, 2019, http://factfinder.census.gov.

35. U.S. Census Bureau, *2013–2017 American Community Survey 5-Year Estimates, Table DP04*, generated by Shawn McMahon, using American FactFinder, accessed July 17, 2019, http://factfinder.census.gov.

36. Pier Village is a Kushner property in nearby Long Branch that has luxury condominiums and high-end, well-known retailers.

37. Reinhart, quoted in "Are Tax Breaks for Developers Good for You?," *Asbury Park Press*, May 3, 2018, https://www.app.com/story/opinion/columnists/2018/05/03/tax-breaks-developers-nj-impact/545778002/.

38. Michelle Gladden, "Springwood Avenue Park Sparks Revitalization," *Asbury Park Sun*, June 20, 2016, http://asburyparksun.com/springwood -avenue-park-opening-sparks-revitalization/.

39. Quoted in Pomorski, "Revitalization Greetings from Asbury Park."

3. Working While Black

1. U.S. Census Bureau, *2008–2012 American Community Survey 5-Year Estimates, Table CP03*, generated by Shawn McMahon using American FactFinder, accessed July 27, 2019, https://factfinder.census.gov; U.S. Census Bureau, *2013–2017 American Community Survey 5-Year Estimates, Table CP03*, generated by Shawn McMahon using American FactFinder, accessed July 27, 2019, http://factfinder.census.gov.

2. John Kain, "Housing Segregation, Negro Employment, and Metropolitan Decentralization," *Quarterly Journal of Economics* 82, no. 2 (1968): 175–197.

3. Keith Ihlanfeldt and David Sjoquist, "The Spatial Mismatch Hypothesis: A Review of Recent Studies and Their Implications for Welfare Reform," *Housing Policy Debate* 9, no. 4 (1998): 851.

4. William Julius Wilson, *The Truly Disadvantaged: The Inner City, the Underclass, and Public Policy* (Chicago: University of Chicago Press, 1987).

5. Rachel Meltzer and Jenny Schuetz, "Bodegas or Bagel Shops? Neighborhood Differences in Retail & Household Services," *Economic Development Quarterly* 26, no. 1 (2012): 73–94; Karen Chapple and Rick Jacobus, "Retail Trade as a Route to Neighborhood Revitalization," in *Urban and Regional Policy and Its Effects*, ed. Nancy Pindus, Howard Wial, and Harold Wolman (Washington, D.C.: Brookings Institution Press, 2009), http://www.jstor.org/stable/10.7864/j.ctt127zb9.

6. Judith K. Hellerstein, David Neumark, and Melissa McInerney, "Spatial Mismatch or Racial Mismatch?," *Journal of Urban Economics* 64, no. 2 (2008): 478.

7. Christopher Mele, *Selling the Lower East Side: Culture, Real Estate, and Resistance in New York City* (Minneapolis: University of Minnesota Press, 2000); Richard Lloyd, *Neo-Bohemia: Art and Commerce in the Postindustrial City* (New York: Routledge, 2006).

8. Arlene Davila, *Barrio Dreams: Puerto Ricans, Latinos, and the Neoliberal City* (Berkeley: University of California Press, 2004).

9. Cailey Rizzo, "Why Asbury Park Is the Coolest Place on the Jersey Shore," *Travel+Leisure*, July 24, 2018, https://www.travelandleisure.com/trip-ideas/beach-vacations/what-to-do-asbury-park.

10. Yasemin Besen-Cassino, "Fun or Exploitation: The Lived Experience of Teenage Employment in Suburban America," *Journal of Contemporary Ethnography* 35, no. 3 (2006): 319–340.

11. Ben Cassleman, "Poor Kids Need Summer Jobs. Rich Kids Get Them," FiveThirtyEight, July 1, 2016, https://fivethirtyeight.com/features/poor-kids-need-summer-jobs-rich-kids-get-them/.

12. Dennis Nickson, Chris Warhurst, and Eli Dutton, "Importance of Attitude and Appearance in the Service Encounter in Retail and Hospitality," *Managing Service Quality* 15, no. 2 (2005): 195–208.

13. Lynne Pettinger, "Brand Culture and Branded Workers: Service Work and Aesthetic Labour in Fashion Retail," *Consumption Markets & Culture* 7, no. 2 (2004): 165–184.

14. Ginia Bellafante, "A Fear Born of Brooklyn Gentrification," *New York Times*, April 9, 2018, https://www.nytimes.com/2018/04/09/nyregion/brooklyn-gentrification-fear-police-shooting.html.

15. Lincoln Quillian, Devah Pager, Ole Hexel, and Arnfinn H. Midtboen, "Meta-analysis of Field Experiments Shows No Change in Racial Discrimination in Hiring over Time," *Proceedings of the National Academies of Sciences* 114, no. 41 (2017): 10870–10875, https://doi.org/10.1073/pnas.1706255114.

16. Connor Maxwell and Danyelle Solomon, "Mass Incarceration, Stress, and Black Infant Mortality: A Case Study in Structural Racism," Center for American Progress, June 5, 2018, https://www.americanprogress.org/issues/race/reports/2018/06/05/451647/mass-incarceration-stress-black-infant-mortality/, 10.

17. Maxwell and Solomon, "Mass Incarceration."

18. NJSA 33:1–25 and NJSA 33:1–26 Criminally Disqualified Licensee.

19. See Andres Mejer Law, "What Is a Crime of Moral Turpitude?," accessed August 2019, https://www.andresmejerlaw.com/discussion -of-crime-of-moral-turpitude-in-monmouth-county-nj/, for a full discussion.

20. Devah Pager and Lincoln Quillian, "Walking the Talk? What Employers Say versus What They Do," *American Sociological Review* 70, no. 3 (2005): 355–380.

21. Robert Cherry and Mary Gatta, "Identifying Effective Prisoner Reentry Strategies," Manhattan Institute, May 2, 2017, https://www.manhattan -institute.org/html/identifying-effective-prisoner-reentry-strategies -10242.html; Marina Duane, Nancy G. La Vigne, Emily Reimal, and Mathew Lynch, *Criminal Background Checks: Impact on Employment and Recidivism* (Washington, D.C.: Urban Institute, 2017), http://www .urban.org/sites/default/files/publication/88621/2017.03.01_criminal _background_checks_report_finalized.pdf.

22. Evelyn Nakano Glenn, "From Servitude to Service Work: Historical Continuities in the Racial Division of Paid Reproduction Labor," *Signs: Journal of Women in Culture and Society* 18, no. 1 (1992): 1–43.

23. Rachel Sherman, *Class Acts: Service and Inequality in Luxury Hotels* (Berkeley: University of California Press, 2006).

24. Maria Heidkamp, Nicole Corre, and Carl Van Horn, "The 'New Unemployables': Older Job Seekers Struggle to Find Work during the Great Recession," Sloan Center on Aging & Work at Boston College, November 2010, http://www.bc.edu/research/agingandwork/archive_pubs/IB25 .html.

25. Yasemin Besen-Cassino, *Consuming Work: Youth Work in America* (Philadelphia: Temple University Press, 2014).

26. U.S. Equal Employment Opportunity Commission, "Abercrombie & Fitch Sued for Religious Discrimination" (press release, September 9, 2010), https://www.eeoc.gov/eeoc/newsroom/release/9-1-10.cfm.

27. Thornhill, quoted in Renee Graham, "When It's OK to Be Black— Just Not Too Black," *Boston Globe*, September 14, 2018, https://www .bostonglobe.com/opinion/2018/09/14/when-black-just-not-too-black/ JWGpAd5802LtQNvXJs3geN/story.html.

28. Chris Warhurst and Dennis Nickson, *Aesthetic Labour* (London: Sage, 2016).

29. Pierre Bourdieu, *Distinction* (London: Routledge, 1984).

30. Jane Goodman and Claire Conway, "Poor Health: When Poverty Becomes Disease," University of California, San Francisco, January 6, 2016, https://www.ucsf.edu/news/2016/01/401251/poor-health-when -poverty-becomes-disease.

31. Bourdieu, *Distinction.*

32. Jean Anyon, *Ghetto Schooling: A Political Economy of Urban Educational Reform* (New York: Teachers College Press, 1997).

33. Sharon Collins, "The Making of the Black Middle Class," *Social Problems* 30, no. 4 (1983): 369–382.

34. Eugene Scott, "Trump's Claim That Black Americans Are Hurt Most by Illegal Immigration Gets Pushback," *Washington Post,* January 9, 2019, https://www.washingtonpost.com/politics/2019/01/09/trumps-claim -that-black-americans-are-hurt-most-by-illegal-immigration-gets -pushback/.

4. Owning a Business

1. Marylin Schlossbach, *Feed This Community: My Life in Food and Community with a Dash of Fun* (self-published manuscript, 2019), https://www .marilynschlossbach.com/cookbook/feed-this-community-cookbook -soft-cover.

2. Liz Jeressi, "Parking and Other Issues Hurting Business Owners in Asbury Park," WJLK, January 8, 2019, https://943thepoint.com/parking -problems-and-other-issues-hurting-business-owners-in-asbury-park/.

3. Beth Greenfield, "Asbury Park's Boardwalk Revival Moves Inward," *New York Times,* February 9, 2011, https://www.nytimes.com/2011/02/09/ realestate/commercial/09asbury.html.

4. Rachel Meltzer, "Gentrification and Small Business: Threat or Opportunity?," *Cityscape* 18, no. 3 (2016): 57–86.

5. Robin DiAngelo, *White Fragility: Why It's So Hard for White People to Talk about Racism* (Boston: Beacon Press, 2018).

6. Abigail Weinberg, "Kirsten Gillibrand Has White Privilege and Knows How to Use It," *Mother Jones,* July 31, 2019, https://www.motherjones .com/politics/2019/07/kirsten-gillibrand-has-white-privilege-and -knows-how-to-use-it/.

7. DiAngelo, *White Fragility.*

8. The Springwood Center is the first building developed under Asbury Park's west side redevelopment plan. It houses a police substation, senior center, Kula Café, training and social service programs, and affordable housing. For more information, see https://gbdmagazine.com/2014/26 -shore-point-architecture/.

9. Chris Pomorski, "Revitalization Greetings from Asbury Park," *Next City,* August 15, 2016, https://nextcity.org/features/view/new-jersey-asbury -park-redevelopment.

10. Austin Bogues, "Asbury Park Salt School Holds Graduation, Fills More Than 70 Jobs," *Asbury Park Press,* April 11, 2019, https://www.app.com/ story/news/local/communitychange/2019/04/11/asbury-park-salt-school -holds-graduation-fills-more-than-70-jobs/3412607002/.

11. Eduardo Bonilla-Silva, *Racism without Racists: Color-Blind Racism and the Persistence of Racial Inequality in the United States* (Lanham, Md.: Rowman & Littlefield, 2010).

12. Matt Huffman and Phillip Cohen, "Racial Wage Inequality: Job Segregation and Devaluation across U.S. Labor Markets," *American Journal of Sociology* 109 (2004): 902–936; Donald Tomaskovic-Devey, *Gender and Racial Inequality at Work* (Ithaca, N.Y.: ILR Press, 1993).

13. M. Bendick, "Situation Testing for Employment Discrimination in the United States of America," *Horizons Stratégiques* 5 (2007): 6–18.

14. Marc Bendick, Rekha Eanni Rodriguez, and Sarumathi Jayaraman, "Employment Discrimination in Upscale Restaurants: Evidence from Matched Pair Testing," *Social Science Journal* 47, no. 4 (2010): 802–818.

15. Reviewed in Philip Moss and Chris Tilly, "Learning about Discrimination by Talking to Employers," in *Handbook on the Economics of Discrimination,* ed. W. Rodgers III (Cheltenham: Edward Elgar, 2006), 61–96. See also Margert Zamudio and Michael Lichter, "Bad Attitudes and Good Soldiers: Soft Skills as a Code for Tractability in the Hiring of Immigrant Latina/os over Native Blacks in the Hotel Industry," *Social Problems* 55 (2008): 573–589.

16. Philip Moss and Chris Tilly, *Stories Employers Tell: Race, Skill, and Hiring in America (Multi-city Study of Urban Inequality)* (New York: Russell Sage Foundation, 2001).

17. Moss and Tilly, "Learning about Discrimination."

18. For example, Moss and Tilly, *Stories Employers Tell*.

19. Moss and Tilly; Rodger Waldinger and Michael Lichter, *How the Other Half Works* (Berkeley: University of California Press, 2003).

20. Chris Warhurst, Chris Tilly, and Mary Gatta, "The New Social Construction of Skills," in *Oxford Handbook of Skills and Training*, ed. John Buchanan, David Finegold, Ken Mayhew, and Chris Warhurst (Oxford: Oxford University Press, 2016), 72–91.

21. Harry Holzer, *What Employers Want* (New York: Russell Sage Foundation, 1996); Harry Holzer and Michael Stoll, "Employer Demand for Welfare Recipients by Race" (JCPR Working Paper 197, Urban Institute, January 1, 2002), https://www.urban.org/research/publication/employer -demand-welfare-recipients-race.

22. Elaine McCrate, "Why Racial Stereotyping Doesn't Just Go Away: The Question of Honesty and Work Ethic" (working paper, Political Economy Research Institute, University of Massachusetts at Amherst, 2006), https://pdfs.semanticscholar.org/45e3/c8faa64c16de8d787c21a- f7e1aa6bb364539.pdf.

23. Pierre Bourdieu, *Distinction* (London: Routledge, 1984).

24. Warhurst, Tilly, and Gatta, "New Social Construction of Skills."

25. Michael Smith, "Abercrombie & Fitch under Fire Again for Cool Kids Comment," *Guardian Express*, May 10, 2013, http://guardianlv.com.

5. A West Side Story

1. Alicia Raia-Hawrylak, "Youth Experiences of Space in a Gentrifying Community: A Case Study of Asbury Park," in *Soul of Society: A Focus on the Lives of Children & Youth*, ed. Mary Nicole Warehime (Bingley, U.K.: Emerald Group, 2014).

2. Paul D'Ambrosio, "Why Should I Pay to Use the Beach?," *Asbury Park Press*, June 11, 2015, https://www.app.com/story/news/local/neptune-wall/ bradley-beach/2015/06/10/nj-beach-badge-fees/71038446/.

3. Tim Hawk and Lori Nichols, "Here's How Much a Beach Badge Costs in Every Jersey Shore Town, 2018 Edition," NJ.com, accessed May 24, 2018, https://www.nj.com/entertainment/2018/05/2018_beach_tag_costs.html.

4. In 2019, Asbury implemented a parking app that could alleviate this issue of change but has other implications around equitable access.

5. Jill Capuzzo, "Man Drowns Trying to Save Boy from Riptide off Asbury Park," *New York Times*, August 2, 2006, https://www.nytimes.com/2006/08/02/nyregion/02drown.html.

6. Associated Press, "Officials Recover Body of Missing N.J. Swimmer in Asbury Park," NJ.com, September 2, 2010, https://www.nj.com/news/2010/09/body_of_missing_swimmer_washes.html.

7. USA Swimming Foundation, "USA Swimming Foundation Announces 5–10% Increase in Swimming Ability among U.S. Children," May 25, 2017, https://www.usaswimmingfoundation.org/utility/landing-pages/news/2017/05/25/usa-swimming-foundation-announces-5-10-percent-increase-in-swimming-ability-among-u.s.-children; Finlo Rohrer, "Why Don't Black Americans Swim?," BBC News, September 3, 2010, https://www.bbc.com/news/world-us-canada-11172054.

8. Cassi Pittman, "Shopping while Black: Black Consumers' Management of Racial Stigma and Racial Profiling in Retail Settings," *Journal of Consumer Culture* 20, no. 1 (2017): 3–22.

9. Elijah Anderson, *StreetWise: Race, Class, and Change in an Urban Community* (Chicago: University of Chicago Press, 1990).

10. Sharon Zukin, *Naked City: The Death and Life of Authentic Urban Places* (New York: Oxford University Press, 2009), 4.

11. D'Ambrosio, "Why Should I Pay?"

12. *Oxford Reference*, s.v., "Thomas Theorem," accessed August 15, 2019, https://www.oxfordreference.com/view/10.1093/oi/authority.20110803104247382.

13. Michelle Gladden, "Community Responds to Excessive Force Report," *Asbury Park Sun*, November 29, 2018, http://asburyparksun.com/community-responds-to-excessive-force-incident/.

14. Sudhir Venkatesh, *American Project: The Rise and Fall of a Modern Ghetto* (Cambridge, Mass.: Harvard University Press, 2000); Sudhir Venkatesh, *Gang Leader for a Day: A Rogue Sociologist Takes to the Streets* (New York: Penguin, 2008).

15. Adam Clark and Carla Astudillo, "See How Your Public School Scores in N.J.'s Newest (and Hidden) Ratings," NJ.com, January 23, 2018, https://www.nj.com/education/2018/01/nj_rated_every_school_on_a_1-100_scale_see_the_res.html.

16. State of New Jersey Department of Education, *New Jersey School Performance Reports 2015–2016 & 2017–2018*, accessed September 2017 and August 1, 2019, https://rc.doe.state.nj.us/report.aspx?County=25& District=0100&School=010&SchoolYear=2015-2016&SY=1516.

17. Center of Budget and Policy Priorities, *Community Eligibility Database: Schools That Can Adopt Community Eligibility for 2015–2016*, accessed July 24, 2019, https://www.cbpp.org/research/food-assistance/community -eligibility-database-schools-that-can-adopt-community-eligibility; Mark Weber and Julia Sass Rubin, "New Jersey Charter Schools: A Data-Driven View—2018 Update, Part I (2018)," Rutgers University Libraries, March 2018, https://doi.org/doi:10.7282/T39Z983M.

18. State of New Jersey Department of Education, *New Jersey School Performance Reports*.

19. John Mooney, "New Education Boss Would Take Seat at Trying Time for State's Schools," NJ Spotlight, January 16, 2018, https://www.nj spotlight.com/stories/18/01/16/new-education-boss-would-take-seat-in -trying-time-for-state-s-schools/.

20. Jean Anyon, *Radical Possibilities: Public Policy, Urban Education, and a New Social Movement* (New York: Routledge, 2005); David C. Berliner, "Our Impoverished View of Educational Research," in *Sociology of Education: A Critical Reader*, ed. Alan Sadovnik and Ryan W. Coughlan (New York: Routledge, 2007), 513–542; Loic Wacquant, *Urban Outcasts: A Comparative Sociology of Advanced Marginality* (Malden, Mass.: Polity Press, 2008); William Julius Wilson, *When Work Disappears: The World of the New Urban Poor* (New York: Vintage, 1997).

21. Jean Anyon, *Ghetto Schooling: A Political Economy of Urban Educational Reform* (New York: Teachers College Press, 1997), 168.

22. Jennifer Burns Stillman, *Gentrification and Schools: The Process of Integration When Whites Reverse Flight* (New York: Palgrave Macmillan, 2012); Mia Bloomfield Cucchiara, *Marketing Schools, Marketing Cities: Who Wins and Who Loses When Schools Become Urban Amenities* (Chicago: University of Chicago Press, 2013); L. Posey-Maddox, *When Middle-Class Parents Choose Urban Schools: Class, Race, and the Challenge of Equity in Public Education* (Chicago: University of Chicago Press, 2014); Francs Pearman II and Walker Swain, "School Choice, Gentrification, and the

Variable Significance of Racial Stratification in Urban Neighborhoods," *Sociology of Education* 90, no. 3 (2017): 213–235.

23. Ester Bloom, "Only 0.1 Percent of US Minimum Wage Workers Can Afford a 1-Bedroom Apartment, Report Finds," CNBC, July 14, 2017, https://www.cnbc.com/2017/07/14/only-point-1-percent-of-us-minimum-wage-workers-can-afford-a-1-bedroom.html.

24. Pearman and Swain, "School Choice"; Molly Vollman Makris, *Public Housing and School Choice in a Gentrified City: Youth Experiences of Uneven Opportunity* (New York: Palgrave Macmillan, 2015); Molly Vollman Makris and Elizabeth Brown, "School Development in Urban Gentrifying Spaces: Developers Supporting Schools or Schools Supporting Developers?," special issue, *Journal of Urban Affairs* (2017), https://doi.org/10.1080/07352166.2017.1360735; Molly Vollman Makris, "The Chimera of Choice: Gentrification, School Choice, and Community," *Peabody Journal of Education* 93, no. 4 (2018): 411–429, https://doi.org/10.1080/0161956X.2018.1488394; Allison Roda, *Inequality in Gifted and Talented Programs: Parental Choices about Status, School Opportunity, and Second-Generation Segregation* (New York: Palgrave Macmillan, 2015).

25. Kfir Mordechay and Jennifer Ayscue, *Could Gentrification Become Integration?*, Civil Rights Project, December 2017, https://www.civilrights project.ucla.edu/research/k-12-education/integration-and-diversity/white-growth-persistent-segregation-could-gentrification-become-integration/DC-Gentrification-122217-km.o.pdf.

26. Liz Jeressi, "5 Monmouth County High Schools Receive Top Nat'l Rankings," WYLK, November 7, 2018, https://943thepoint.com/five-of-monmouth-countys-high-school-receive-top-national-rankings/.

27. State of New Jersey Department of Education, *New Jersey School Performance Reports*.

28. Laura Waters, "Are We Getting What We Paid for in Asbury Park Schools?," WHYY, December 3, 2014, https://whyy.org/articles/are-we-getting-what-we-paid-for-in-asbury-park-schools/; Tom Davis, "Taxpayers in the NJ Districts Pay More Than Anybody," Patch, June 2, 2019, https://Patch/new-jersey/tomsriver/taxpayers-these-300-nj-school-districts-pay-more-anybody; Tom Davis, "Asbury Park Pays This Much to Send Kids to School," Patch, June 5, 2019, https://patch.com/new

-jersey/asbury-park/asbury-park-pays-much-send-kids-school; Joe
Strupp, "Asbury Park Schools per Pupil Spending Tops Jersey Shore List
Again, Up $5k Each," *Asbury Park Press*, August 9, 2019, https://www
.app.com/story/news/education/in-our-schools/2019/08/09/asbury-park
-schools-per-pupil-spending-tops-jersey-shore-list-again/1954710001/.

29. Makris, *Public Housing and School Choice*; Elizabeth Brown and
Molly Makris Vollman, "A Different Type of Charter School: In
Prestige Charters a Rise in Cachet Equals a Decline in Access," *Journal
of Education Policy* 33, no. 1 (2017): 85–117, http://dx.doi.org/10.1080/
02680939.2017.1341552.

30. Pauline Lipman, *The New Political Economy of Urban Education: Neoliberalism, Race, and the Right to the City* (New York: Routledge, 2011).

31. Lipman; Eve Ewing, *Ghosts in the Schoolyard: Racism and School Closings
on Chicago's South Side* (Chicago: University of Chicago Press, 2018).

32. Makris and Brown, "School Development."

33. Makris, *Public Housing and School Choice*; Makris and Brown, "School
Development."

34. U.S. Census Bureau, *Census 2000 Summary File 1, Table DP-1*, generated
by Shawn McMahon, using American FactFinder, accessed July 16, 2019,
https://factfinder.census.gov; U.S. Census Bureau, *2013–2017 American
Community Survey 5-Year Estimates, Table S0101*, generated by Shawn
McMahon, using American FactFinder, accessed June 20, 2019, http://
factfinder.census.gov.

35. Kriston Capps, "Are Dog Parks Exclusionary?," CityLab, February 28,
2019, https://www.citylab.com/equity/2019/02/chicago-dog-park-lincoln
-yards-gentrification-racial-divide/581086/.

36. David Hyra, *Race, Class, and Politics in the Cappuccino City* (Chicago:
University of Chicago Press, 2017).

37. At the time of our interview, Chris Christie, who had been the gover-
nor of New Jersey (for eight years), had been out of office for about six
months. The mayor of Asbury Park at the time was John Moor.

6. Cats Are the New Dogs

1. John Bazley, "Asbury Lanes Should Stay Closed: Bazley," *Asbury Park Press*, March 17, 2018, https://www.app.com/story/opinion/columnists/2018/03/17/asbury-lanes-reopening-asbury-park/434850002/.

2. Bazley.

3. Jessica Glenza, "New Jersey Town Made Famous by Springsteen at Centre of Gentrification Row," *Guardian*, June 17, 2018, https://www.theguardian.com/us-news/2018/jun/17/bruce-springsteen-asbury-park-new-jersey.

4. Arlene Davila, *Barrio Dreams: Puerto Ricans, Latinos, and the Neoliberal City* (Berkeley: University of California Press, 2004).

5. Christopher Mele, *Selling the Lower East Side: Culture, Real Estate, and Resistance in New York City* (Minneapolis: University of Minnesota Press, 2000).

6. Jeremiah Moss, *Vanishing New York: How a Great City Lost Its Soul* (New York: Dey Street Books, 2017).

7. Sharon Zukin, *Naked City: The Death and Life of Authentic Urban Places* (New York: Oxford University Press, 2009).

8. Richard L. Florida, *The Rise of the Creative Class: And How It's Transforming Work, Leisure, Community and Everyday Life* (New York: Basic Books, 2002).

9. Florida, *Rise of the Creative Class*.

10. Sabina Mollot, "City Council Debates Retails 'High Rent Blight' Dilemma," *Real Estate Weekly*, October 21, 2016, https://rew-online.com/2016/10/city-council-high-rent-blight-retail/.

11. D. Thompson, "How Manhattan Became a Rich Ghost Town," *Atlantic*, October 15, 2018, https://www.theatlantic.com/ideas/archive/2018/10/new-york-retail-vacancy/572911/.

12. *Timbs* refers to Timberland boots.

13. Antonia Randolph, *The Wrong Kind of Different: Challenging the Meaning of Diversity in American Classrooms* (New York: Teachers College Press, 2013).

14. Jason Hackworth, "Postrecession Gentrification in New York City," *Urban Affairs Review* 37 (2002): 815–843, https://journals.sagepub.com/doi/10.1177/107874037006003; Loretta Lees, "Super-gentrification: The

Case of Brooklyn Heights, New York City," *Urban Studies* 40 (2003): 2487–2509.

15. Peter Marcuse, "The Enclave, the Citadel, and the Ghetto: What Has Changed in the Post-Fordist U.S. City," *Urban Affairs Review* 33, no. 2 (1997): 228–264.

16. Heidelberg Project, "History," accessed August 2019, https://www.heidelberg.org/history.

7. Land of Hope and Dreams?

1. Dana Schulz, "Asbury Park's Second Act: How Developer iStar Is Transforming This Jersey Shore Town," 6SQFT, July 26, 2019, https://www.6sqft.com/asbury-parks-second-act-how-developer-istar-is-transforming-this-jersey-shore-town/.

2. Michelle Gladden, "Mayor Confirms Shooting along AP Boardwalk," *Asbury Park Sun*, July 5, 2019, http://asburyparksun.com/mayor-confirms-shooting-along-ap-boardwalk/?fbclid=IwAR18V7XtjrNcV_xrC_t2T9pxzysCMGtqICgZ7R-_UtGYhBToRetCGtlxW7U.

3. Tom Davis, "2 Shot on Asbury Park Boardwalk after July 4th Fireworks," Patch, July 5, 2019, https://Patch/new-jersey/asbury-park/2-shot-asbury-park-boardwalk-after-july-4-fireworks-mcpo.

4. Gladden, "Mayor Confirms Shooting."

5. Mark Sundstrom, "Fatal Police Officer-Involved Shooting in Asbury Park, NJ Reports," WPIX, July 24, 2019, https://pix11.com/2019/07/24/fatal-police-officer-involved-shooting-in-asbury-park-reports/; RLS Media, "Life Threatening Injuries Reported for Victim of Sewall Avenue Shooting in Asbury Park," July 24, 2019, https://www.rlsmedia.com/article/life-threatening-injuries-reported-victim-sewall-avenue-shooting-asbury-park.

6. Zillow, "Economic Data," accessed July 18, 2019, https://www.zillow.com/research/data/.

7. Among the remaining five are three Hudson County cities and two Cape May County cities.

8. Michelle Gladden, "Community Responds to Excessive Force Report," *Asbury Park Sun*, November 29, 2018, http://asburyparksun.com/community-responds-to-excessive-force-incident/.

9. Council of New Jersey Grantmakers, "Wells Fargo Investing in Asbury Park," August 21, 2018, https://www.cnjg.org/news/wells-fargo-investing -asbury-park-s-west-side.

10. David Hyra, *Race, Class, and Politics in the Cappuccino City* (Chicago: University of Chicago Press, 2017).

11. Tanvi Misra, "Gentrification Doesn't Mean Diversity," CityLab, May 17, 2017, https://www.citylab.com/equity/2017/05/gentrifying-neighbor hoods-arent-really-diverse/526092/.

12. PDR Edge, "Vienna's Unique Social Housing Program," accessed December 2019, https://www.huduser.gov/portal/pdredge/pdr_edge _featd_article_011314.html.

13. David Price, "7 Policies That Could Prevent Gentrification," Shelterforce, May 23, 2014, https://shelterforce.org/2014/05/23/7_policies_that_could _prevent_gentrification/.

14. U.S. Census Bureau, *2013–2017 American Community Survey 5-Year Estimates, Table S0101*, generated by Shawn McMahon, using American FactFinder, accessed June 20, 2019, http://factfinder.census.gov.

15. U.S. Census Bureau, *2013–2017 American Community Survey 5-Year Estimates, Table DP04*, generated by Shawn McMahon, using American FactFinder, accessed July 17, 2019, http://factfinder.census.gov.

16. Regina Clewlow, "DC Is Growing Its Dockless Bike and Scooter Program: We Partnered with Them to Evaluate How It's Expanding Access in Underserved Communities," Medium, November 15, 2018, https:// medium.com/populus-ai/measuring-equity-dockles.

17. Asbury does have shuttles sponsored by those in the hospitality sector, but when you take one, it is clear that the drivers earn their money from tips and that these are focused on making the entire West Side accessible for tourists, not bridging the east and west sides. In addition, nearby Long Branch, New Jersey, implemented free beach parking for residents in 2019. For details, see Josh Bakan, "Long Branch Residents Get Free Beachfront Parking," Patch, May 9, 2019, https://Patch/new-jersey/ longbranch/long-branch-residents-get-free-beachfront-parking.

18. For a chart of New Jersey minimum wage increases, see https://www.nj .gov/labor/forms_pdfs/wagehour/minimumwage_postcard.pdf.

19. Lindsey Miller, "We Need to Change How We Think about Gentrification," *National Civic Review* 107, no. 4 (2019), https://www.national

civicleague.org/ncr-article/we-need-to-change-how-we-think-about
-gentrification/.

20. Chris Pomorski, "Revitalization Greetings from Asbury Park," *Next City*, August 15, 2016, https://nextcity.org/features/view/new-jersey-asbury -park-redevelopment.

Methodological Appendix

1. Alicia Raia-Hawrylak, "Youth Experiences of Space in a Gentrifying Community: A Case Study of Asbury Park," in *Soul of Society: A Focus on the Lives of Children & Youth*, ed. Mary Nicole Warehime (Bingley, U.K.: Emerald Group, 2014); Chris Pomorski, "Revitalization Greetings from Asbury Park," *Next City*, August 15, 2016, https://nextcity.org/features/ view/new-jersey-asbury-park-redevelopment.

Bibliography

Anderson, Elijah. *StreetWise: Race, Class, and Change in an Urban Community*. Chicago: University of Chicago Press, 1990.

Andres Mejer Law. "What Is a Crime of Moral Turpitude?" Accessed August 2019. https://www.andresmejerlaw.com/discussion-of-crime-of-moral-turpitude-in-monmouth-county-nj/.

Anyon, Jean. *Ghetto Schooling: A Political Economy of Urban Educational Reform*. New York: Teachers College Press, 1997.

———. *Radical Possibilities: Public Policy, Urban Education, and a New Social Movement*. New York: Routledge, 2005.

Argent, Neil, Matthew Tonts, Roy Jones, and John Holmes. "A Creativity-Led Rural Renaissance? Amenity-Led Migration, the Creative Turn and the Uneven Development of Rural Australia." *Applied Geography* 44 (2013): 88–98.

Asbury Ocean Club. "Asbury Ocean Club Amenities." Accessed August 2019. https://asburyoceanclub.com/amenities/.

Asbury Park Press. "Are Tax Breaks for Developers Good for You?" May 3, 2018. https://www.app.com/story/opinion/columnists/2018/05/03/tax-breaks-developers-nj-impact/545778002/.

Associated Press. "Officials Recover Body of Missing N.J. Swimmer in Asbury Park." NJ.com, September 2, 2010. https://www.nj.com/news/2010/09/body_of_missing_swimmer_washes.html.

Bagli, Charles. "Asbury Park Long Neglected Shows Signs of Rejuvenation." *New York Times*, August 1, 2015. https://www.nytimes.com/2015/08/01/nyregion/asbury-park-long-neglected-shows-signs-of-rejuvenation.html.

Bazley, John. "Asbury Lanes Should Stay Closed: Bazley." *Asbury Park Press*, March 17, 2018. https://www.app.com/story/opinion/columnists/2018/03/17/asbury-lanes-reopening-asbury-park/434850002/.

——. "Long Branch Residents Get Free Beachfront Parking." Patch, May 9, 2019. https://Patch/new-jersey/longbranch/long-branch-residents-get-free-beachfront-parking.

Bellafante, Ginia. "A Fear Born of Brooklyn Gentrification." *New York Times*, April 9, 2018. https://www.nytimes.com/2018/04/09/nyregion/brooklyn-gentrification-fear-police-shooting.html.

Bendick, Marc. "Situation Testing for Employment Discrimination in the United States of America." *Horizons Stratégiques* 5 (2007): 6–18.

Bendick, Marc, Rekha Eanni Rodriguez, and Sarumathi Jayaraman. "Employment Discrimination in Upscale Restaurants: Evidence from Matched Pair Testing." *Social Science Journal* 47, no. 4 (2010): 802–818.

Berliner, David C. "Our Impoverished View of Educational Research." In *Sociology of Education: A Critical Reader*, edited by Alan Sadovnik and Ryan W. Coughlan, 513–542. New York: Routledge, 2007.

Berry, Brian J. "Islands of Renewal in Seas of Decay." In *The New Urban Reality*, by Brian J. Berry, edited by Paul E. Peterson, 69–96. Washington, D.C.: Brookings Institute, 1985.

Besen-Cassino, Yasemin. *Consuming Work: Youth Work in America*. Philadelphia: Temple University Press, 2014.

——. "Fun or Exploitation: The Lived Experience of Teenage Employment in Suburban America." *Journal of Contemporary Ethnography* 35, no. 3 (2006): 319–340.

Besonen, Julie. "Asbury Park: Where Art, Grit, and Local Spirits Mix." *New York Times*, August 4, 2017. https://www.nytimes.com/2017/08/04/nyregion/asbury-park.html.

Bloom, Ester. "Only 0.1 Percent of US Minimum Wage Workers Can Afford a 1-Bedroom Apartment, Report Finds." CNBC, July 14, 2017. https://www.cnbc.com/2017/07/14/only-point-1-percent-of-us-minimum-wage-workers-can-afford-a-1-bedroom.html.

Bogues, Austin. "Asbury Park Bans Smoking at the Beaches." *Asbury Park Press*, April 27, 2018. https://www.app.com/story/news/local/community change/2018/04/27/asbury-park-bans-smoking-beaches/557837002/.

————. "Asbury Park Salt School Holds Graduation, Fills More Than 70 Jobs." *Asbury Park Press*, April 11, 2019. https://www.app.com/story/ news/local/communitychange/2019/04/11/asbury-park-salt-school-holds -graduation-fills-more-than-70-jobs/3412607002/.

————. "Esperanza Site Renamed Asbury Ocean Club Surfside Resort and Residences." *Asbury Park Press*, May 9, 2018. https://www.app.com/story/ news/local/communitychange/2018/05/09/asbury-park-esperanza-site -renamed-asbury-ocean-club/592837002/.

————. "In 1968, Music Saved Asbury Park." *Asbury Park Press*, July 10, 2018. https://www.app.com/story/entertainment/2018/07/10/1968-music-saved -asbury-park/632729002/.

Bogues, Austin, and Ryan Ross. "Asbury Park Ranked among 50 Worst United States Cities to Live In." *Asbury Park Press*, February 7, 2019. https://www.app.com/story/news/local/how-we-live/2019/02/07/asbury -park-worst-united-states-cities/2800228002/.

Bonilla-Silva, Eduardo. *Racism without Racists: Color-Blind Racism and the Persistence of Racial Inequality in the United States*. Lanham, Md.: Rowman & Littlefield, 2010.

Bourdieu, Pierre. *Distinction*. London: Routledge, 1984.

Brown, Elizabeth, and Molly Makris Vollman. "A Different Type of Charter School: In Prestige Charters a Rise in Cachet Equals a Decline in Access." *Journal of Education Policy* 33, no. 1 (2017): 85–117. http://dx.doi .org/10.1080/02680939.2017.1341552.

Brown-Saracino, Japonica. *The Gentrification Debates*. New York: Routledge, 2010.

Capps, Kriston. "Are Dog Parks Exclusionary?" CityLab, February 28, 2019. https://www.citylab.com/equity/2019/02/chicago-dog-park-lincoln -yards-gentrification-racial-divide/581086/.

Capuzzo, Jill P. "Asbury Park's Long Recovery." *New York Times*, December 7, 2003. https://www.nytimes.com/2003/12/07/nyregion/asbury-park -s-long-recovery.html.

————. "Man Drowns Trying to Save Boy from Riptide off Asbury Park." *New York Times*, August 2, 2006. https://www.nytimes.com/2006/08/02/ nyregion/o2drown.html.

Cassleman, Ben. "Poor Kids Need Summer Jobs. Rich Kids Get Them." FiveThirtyEight, July 1, 2016. https://fivethirtyeight.com/features/poor -kids-need-summer-jobs-rich-kids-get-them/.

Center of Budget and Policy Priorities. *Community Eligibility Database: Schools That Can Adopt Community Eligibility for 2015–2016.* Accessed July 24, 2019. https://www.cbpp.org/research/food-assistance/community -eligibility-database-schools-that-can-adopt-community-eligibility.

Chapple, Karen, and Rick Jacobus. "Retail Trade as a Route to Neighborhood Revitalization." In *Urban and Regional Policy and Its Effects,* edited by Nancy Pindus, Howard Wial, and Harold Wolman. Brookings Institution Press, 2009. http://www.jstor.org/stable/10.7864/j.ctt127zb9.

Cherry, Robert, and Mary Gatta. "Identifying Effective Prisoner Reentry Strategies." Manhattan Institute, May 2, 2017. https://www.manhattan -institute.org/html/identifying-effective-prisoner-reentry-strategies -10242.html.

Christafore, David, and Susane Leguizamon. "Is 'Gaytrification' a Real Phenomenon?" *Urban Affairs Review* 54, no. 5 (2018). https://doi.org/10 .1177/1078087416682321.

Clark, Adam, and Carla Astudillo. "See How Your Public School Scores in N.J.'s Newest (and Hidden) Ratings." NJ.com, January 23, 2018. https:// www.nj.com/education/2018/01/nj_rated_every_school_on_a_1-100 _scale_see_the_res.html.

Clewlow, Regina. "DC Is Growing Its Dockless Bike and Scooter Program: We Partnered with Them to Evaluate How It's Expanding Access in Underserved Communities." Medium, November 15, 2018. https:// medium.com/populus-ai/measuring-equity-dockles.

Coleman, Tennyson. "How Asbury Park's Paradise Became One of the Oldest (but Still Hottest) Gay Club in N.J." NJ.com, July 2, 2019. https:// www.nj.com/entertainment/2019/06/heres-how-asbury-parks-paradise -became-the-oldest-but-still-hottest-gay-club-in-nj.html.

Collins, Sharon. "The Making of the Black Middle Class." *Social Problems* 30, no. 4 (1983): 369–382.

Council of New Jersey Grantmakers. "Wells Fargo Investing in Asbury Park." August 21, 2018. https://www.cnjg.org/news/wells-fargo-investing -asbury-park-s-west-side.

Crenshaw, Kimberle. "Demarginalizing the Intersection of Race and Sex: A Black Feminist Critique of Antidiscrimination Doctrine, Feminist Theory and Antiracist Politics." *University of Chicago Legal Forum* 1989 (1989). https://chicagounbound.uchicago.edu/uclf/vol1989/iss1/8/.

Cucchiara, Mia Bloomfield. *Marketing Schools, Marketing Cities: Who Wins and Who Loses When Schools Become Urban Amenities*. Chicago: University of Chicago Press, 2013.

Curran, Winifred. "Gentrification and the Nature of Work: Exploring the Links in Williamsburg, Brooklyn." *Environment and Planning* 36 (2004): 1243–1258.

D'Ambrosio, Paul. "Why Should I Pay to Use the Beach?" *Asbury Park Press*, June 11, 2015. https://www.app.com/story/news/local/neptune-wall/ bradley-beach/2015/06/10/nj-beach-badge-fees/71038446/.

Darling, Eliza. "The City in the Country: Wilderness Gentrification and the Rent Gap." *Environment and Planning A: Economy and Space* 37, no. 6 (2005): 1015–1032. https://doi.org/10.1068/a37158.

Davila, Arlene. *Barrio Dreams: Puerto Ricans, Latinos, and the Neoliberal City*. Berkeley: University of California Press, 2004.

Davis, Tom. "Asbury Park Pays This Much to Send Kids to School." Patch, June 5, 2019. https://patch.com/new-jersey/asbury-park/asbury-park -pays-much-send-kids-school.

———. "Taxpayers in the NJ Districts Pay More Than Anybody." Patch, June 2, 2019. https://Patch/new-jersey/tomsriver/taxpayers-these-300-nj -school-districts-pay-more-anybody.

———. "2 Shot on Asbury Park Boardwalk after July 4th Fireworks." Patch, July 5, 2019. https://Patch/new-jersey/asbury-park/2-shot-asbury-park -boardwalk-after-july-4-fireworks-mcpo.

DiAngelo, Robin. *White Fragility: Why It's So Hard for White People to Talk about Racism*. Boston: Beacon Press, 2018.

Duane, Marina, Nancy G. La Vigne, Emily Reimal, and Mathew Lynch. *Criminal Background Checks: Impact on Employment and Recidivism*. Washington, D.C.: Urban Institute, 2017. http://www.urban.org/sites/ default/files/publication/88621/2017.03.01_criminal_background_checks _report_finalized.pdf.

Durso, Laura, and Gary Gates. *Serving Our Youth: Findings from a National Survey of Service Providers Working with Lesbian, Gay, Bisexual, and Transgender Youth Who Are Homeless or At Risk of Becoming Homeless*. Los Angeles: Williams Institute, 2012.

Epstein, Dan. "Bruce Springsteen's 'Greetings from Asbury Park, N.J.': 10 Things You Didn't Know." *Rolling Stone*, January 5, 2018. https://www

.rollingstone.com/music/music-news/bruce-springsteens-greetings-from
-asbury-park-n-j-10-things-you-didnt-know-204206/.

Ewing, Eve. *Ghosts in the Schoolyard: Racism and School Closings on Chicago's South Side*. Chicago: University of Chicago Press, 2018.

Federal Housing Finance Agency. "National Mortgage Database." Accessed June 22, 2019. https://www.fhfa.gov/PolicyProgramsResearch/Programs/Pages/National-Mortgage-Database.aspx.

Ferrell, Jeff. *Tearing Down the Streets: Adventures in Urban Anarchy*. New York: Palgrave Macmillan, 2002.

Firpo-Cappiellois, Robert. "Meet the Coolest Small Town in America." *Budget Travel*, June 2, 2017. https://www.budgettravel.com/article/meet-the-coolest-small-town-in-america-2017.

Florida, Richard. "Cities and the Creative Class." *City and Community* 2, no. 1 (2003): 3–18. https://doi.org/10.1111/1540-6040.00034.

———. *The Rise of the Creative Class: And How It's Transforming Work, Leisure, Community and Everyday Life*. New York: Basic Books, 2002.

Freeman, Lance. *There Goes the "Hood": Views of Gentrification from the Ground Up*. Philadelphia: Temple University Press, 2006.

Ghaziani, Amin. *There Goes the Gayborhood?* Princeton, N.J.: Princeton University Press, 2014.

Gladden, Michelle. "Community Responds to Excessive Force Report." *Asbury Park Sun*, November 29, 2018. http://asburyparksun.com/community-responds-to-excessive-force-incident/.

———. "Mayor Confirms Shooting along AP Boardwalk." *Asbury Park Sun*, July 5, 2019. http://asburyparksun.com/mayor-confirms-shooting-along-ap-boardwalk/?fbclid=IwAR18V7XtjrNcV_xrC_t2T9pxzysCMGtqIC gZ7R-_UtGYhBToRetCGtlxW7U.

———. "Springwood Avenue Park Sparks Revitalization." *Asbury Park Sun*, June 20, 2016. http://asburyparksun.com/springwood-avenue-park-opening-sparks-revitalization/.

———. "Update: Asbury Galleria Owner Forced to Close Boardwalk Shop." *Asbury Park Sun*, January 17, 2018. http://asburyparksun.com/asbury-galleria-owner-forced-to-close-boardwalk-venture/.

Glenza, Jessica. "New Jersey Town Made Famous by Springsteen at Centre of Gentrification Row." *Guardian*, June 17, 2018. https://www.the

guardian.com/us-news/2018/jun/17/bruce-springsteen-asbury-park-new
-jersey.

Goldberg, David. "Greetings from Jim Crow, New Jersey: Contesting the
Meaning and Abandonment of Reconstruction in the Public and Commercial Spaces of Asbury Park, 1880–1890." *Concept* 30 (2007). https://
concept.journals.villanova.edu/article/view/279.

———. *The Retreats of Reconstruction*. New York: Fordham University Press,
2017.

Goodman, Jane, and Claire Conway. "Poor Health: When Poverty Becomes
Disease." University of California, San Francisco, January 6, 2016.
https://www.ucsf.edu/news/2016/01/401251/poor-health-when-poverty
-becomes-disease.

Graham, Renee. "When It's OK to Be Black—Just Not Too Black." *Boston
Globe*, September 14, 2018. https://www.bostonglobe.com/opinion/2018/
09/14/when-black-just-not-too-black/JWGpAd5802LtQNvXJs3geN/
story.html.

Greenfield, Beth. "Asbury Park's Boardwalk Revival Moves Inward." *New
York Times*, February 9, 2011. https://www.nytimes.com/2011/02/09/
realestate/commercial/09asbury.html.

Hackworth, Jason. "Postrecession Gentrification in New York City." *Urban
Affairs Review* 37 (2002): 815–843. https://journals.sagepub.com/doi/10
.1177/107874037006003.

Hawk, Tim, and Lori Nichols. "Here's How Much a Beach Badge Costs in
Every Jersey Shore Town, 2018 Edition." NJ.com. Accessed May 24, 2018.
https://www.nj.com/entertainment/2018/05/2018_beach_tag_costs.html.

Heidelberg Project. "History." Accessed August 2019. https://www.heidel
berg.org/history.

Heidkamp, Maria, Nicole Corre, and Carl Van Horn. "The 'New Unemployables': Older Job Seekers Struggle to Find Work during the Great
Recession." Sloan Center on Aging & Work at Boston College, November 2010. http://www.bc.edu/research/agingandwork/archive_pubs/IB25
.html.

Hellerstein, Judith K., David Neumark, and Melissa McInerney. "Spatial
Mismatch or Racial Mismatch?" *Journal of Urban Economics* 64, no. 2
(2008): 464–479.

Holzer, Harry. *What Employers Want*. New York: Russell Sage Foundation, 1996.

Holzer, Harry, and Michael Stoll. "Employer Demand for Welfare Recipients by Race." JCPR Working Paper 197, Urban Institute, January 1, 2002. https://www.urban.org/research/publication/employer-demand -welfare-recipients-race.

Huffman, Matt, and Phillip Cohen. "Racial Wage Inequality: Job Segregation and Devaluation across U.S. Labor Markets." *American Journal of Sociology* 109 (2004): 902–936.

Hyra, David. *Race, Class, and Politics in the Cappuccino City*. Chicago: University of Chicago Press, 2017.

Ihlanfeldt, Keith, and David Sjoquist. "The Spatial Mismatch Hypothesis: A Review of Recent Studies and Their Implications for Welfare Reform." *Housing Policy Debate* 9, no. 4 (1998): 849–892.

Jacobson, Dan. "Time to Honor Historic LGBT Moment in Asbury Park." *triCityNews*, August 22, 2019.

James, Scott. "There Goes the Gayborhood." *New York Times*, June 21, 2017. https://www.nytimes.com/2017/06/21/us/gay-pride-lgbtq-gayborhood .html.

Jeressi, Liz. "5 Monmouth County High Schools Receive Top Nat'l Rankings." WYLK, November 7, 2018. https://943thepoint.com/five-of -monmouth-countys-high-school-receive-top-national-rankings/.

———. "Parking and Other Issues Hurting Business Owners in Asbury Park." WJLK, January 8, 2019. https://943thepoint.com/parking -problems-and-other-issues-hurting-business-owners-in-asbury-park/.

Jordan, C. "Bruce Springsteen Dances with His Mom at Wonder Bar to Celebrate Her Birthday." *Asbury Park Press*, April 15, 2018. https://www .app.com/story/entertainment/music/2018/04/15/bruce-springsteen -dances-mom-wonder-bar-celebrate-her-birthday/519361002/.

———. "Judy Garland's Really Bad Week at the Jersey Shore." *Asbury Park Press*, June 26, 2018. https://www.app.com/story/entertainment/music/ 2018/06/26/judy-garlands-really-bad-week-jersey-shore-50th-year -anniversary/734441002/.

Kain, John. "Housing Segregation, Negro Employment, and Metropolitan Decentralization." *Quarterly Journal of Economics* 82, no. 2 (1968): 175–197.

Kolko, Jed. "Job Location, Neighborhood Change, and Gentrification." Working paper, Public Policy Institute of California, 2009. https://dx.doi.org/10.2139/ssrn.1662548.

Lees, Loretta. "Super-gentrification: The Case of Brooklyn Heights, New York City." *Urban Studies* 40 (2003): 2487–2509.

Lester, T. William, and Daniel Hartley. "The Long Term Employment Impacts of Gentrification in the 1990s." *Regional Science and Urban Economics* 45 (2014): 80–89.

Ley, David. *The New Middle Class and the Remaking of the Central City.* Oxford: Oxford University Press, 1996.

Lipman, Pauline. *The New Political Economy of Urban Education: Neoliberalism, Race, and the Right to the City.* New York: Routledge, 2011.

Lloyd, Richard. *Neo-Bohemia: Art and Commerce in the Postindustrial City.* New York: Routledge, 2006.

Makris, Molly Vollman. "The Chimera of Choice: Gentrification, School Choice, and Community." *Peabody Journal of Education* 93, no. 4 (2018): 411–429. https://doi.org/10.1080/0161956X.2018.1488394.

———. *Public Housing and School Choice in a Gentrified City: Youth Experiences of Uneven Opportunity.* New York: Palgrave Macmillan, 2015.

Makris, Molly Vollman, and Elizabeth Brown. "School Development in Urban Gentrifying Spaces: Developers Supporting Schools or Schools Supporting Developers?" Special issue, *Journal of Urban Affairs* (2017). https://doi.org/10.1080/07352166.2017.1360735.

Marcuse, Peter. "The Enclave, the Citadel, and the Ghetto: What Has Changed in the Post-Fordist U.S. City." *Urban Affairs Review* 33, no. 2 (1997): 228–264.

Martin, Katrina. "The Asbury Park July 1970 Riots." *Devil's Tale* (blog), Duke University Libraries, June 28, 2016. https://blogs.library.duke.edu/rubenstein/2016/06/28/asbury-park-july-1970-riots/.

Maxwell, Connor, and Danyelle Solomon. "Mass Incarceration, Stress, and Black Infant Mortality: A Case Study in Structural Racism." Center for American Progress, June 5, 2018. https://www.americanprogress.org/issues/race/reports/2018/06/05/451647/mass-incarceration-stress-black-infant-mortality/.

McCrate, Elaine. "Why Racial Stereotyping Doesn't Just Go Away: The Question of Honesty and Work Ethic." Working paper, Political

Economy Research Institute, University of Massachusetts at Amherst, 2006. https://pdfs.semanticscholar.org/45e3/c8faa64c16de8d787c21a f7e1aa6bb364539.pdf.

McMullen, Troy. "Historically Black Beach Enclaves Are Fighting to Save Their History and Identity." *Washington Post*, July 7, 2017. https://www .washingtonpost.com/realestate/surf-sand-and-race/2017/07/26/f674c5be -61bb-11e7-84a1-a26b75ad39fe_story.html.

Mele, Christopher. *Selling the Lower East Side: Culture, Real Estate, and Resistance in New York City*. Minneapolis: University of Minnesota Press, 2000.

Meltzer, Rachel. "Gentrification and Small Business: Threat or Opportunity?" *Cityscape* 18, no. 3 (2016): 57–86.

Meltzer, Rachel, and Pooya Ghorbani. "Does Gentrification Increase Employment Opportunities in Low-Income Neighborhoods?" *Regional Science and Urban Economics* 66 (2017): 52–73.

Meltzer, Rachel, and Jenny Schuetz. "Bodegas or Bagel Shops? Neighborhood Differences in Retail & Household Services." *Economic Development Quarterly* 26, no. 1 (2012): 73–94.

Mikie, Jean. "U2 Played Twice at This Legendary Asbury Park Club." *Asbury Park Press*, November 9, 2014. https://www.app.com/story/news/local/ eatontown-asbury-park/asbury-park/2014/11/09/u-played-twice -legendary-asbury-park-club/18756973/.

Miller, Lindsey. "We Need to Change How We Think about Gentrification." *National Civic Review* 107, no. 4 (2019). https://www.national civicleague.org/ncr-article/we-need-to-change-how-we-think-about -gentrification/.

Misra, Tanvi. "Gentrification Doesn't Mean Diversity." May 17, 2017. https:// www.citylab.com/equity/2017/05/gentrifying-neighborhoods-arent-really -diverse/526092/.

Mollot, Sabina. "City Council Debates Retails 'High Rent Blight' Dilemma." *Real Estate Weekly*, October 21, 2016. https://rew-online.com/ 2016/10/city-council-high-rent-blight-retail/.

Mooney, John. "New Education Boss Would Take Seat at Trying Time for State's Schools." NJ Spotlight, January 16, 2018. https://www.njspotlight .com/stories/18/01/16/new-education-boss-would-take-seat-in-trying -time-for-state-s-schools/.

Mordechay, Kfir, and Jennifer Ayscue. *Could Gentrification Become Integration?* Civil Rights Project, December 2017. https://www.civilrightsproject.ucla.edu/research/k-12-education/integration-and-diversity/white-growth-persistent-segregation-could-gentrification-become-integration/DC-Gentrification-122217-km.o.pdf.

Moss, Jeremiah. *Vanishing New York: How a Great City Lost Its Soul.* New York: Dey Street Books, 2017.

Moss, Laurence A. G. *The Amenity Migrants: Seeking and Sustaining Mountains and Their Cultures.* Oxfordshire, U.K.: CAB International North America, 2006.

Moss, Philip, and Chris Tilly. "Learning about Discrimination by Talking to Employers." In *Handbook on the Economics of Discrimination,* edited by W. Rodgers III, 61–96. Cheltenham: Edward Elgar, 2006.

———. *Stories Employers Tell: Race, Skill, and Hiring in America (Multi-city Study of Urban Inequality).* New York: Russell Sage Foundation, 2001.

Nakano Glenn, Evelyn. "From Servitude to Service Work: Historical Continuities in the Racial Division of Paid Reproduction Labor." *Signs: Journal of Women in Culture and Society* 18, no. 1 (1992): 1–43.

Newman, Kathe, and Elvin Wyly. "The Right to Stay Put, Revisited: Gentrification and Resistance to Displacement in New York City." *Urban Studies* 43, no. 1 (2006): 44–52. https://doi.org/10.1080/0042 0980500388710.

Nickson, Dennis, Chris Warhurst, and Eli Dutton. "Importance of Attitude and Appearance in the Service Encounter in Retail and Hospitality." *Managing Service Quality* 15, no. 2 (2005): 195–208.

Oxford Reference. s.v. "Thomas Theorem." Accessed August 15, 2019. https://www.oxfordreference.com/view/10.1093/oi/authority.20110803104247382.

Pager, Devah, and Lincoln Quillian. "Walking the Talk? What Employers Say versus What They Do." *American Sociological Review* 70, no. 3 (2005): 355–380.

Paris, Chris. "Re-positioning Second Homes within Housing Studies: Household Investment, Gentrification, Multiple Residence, Mobility and Hyper-consumption." *Housing Theory and Society* 26, no. 4 (2009): 292–310.

Patillo, Mary. *Black on the Block.* Chicago: University of Chicago Press, 2008.

PDR Edge. "Vienna's Unique Social Housing Program." Accessed December 2019. https://www.huduser.gov/portal/pdredge/pdr_edge_featd _article_011314.html.

Pearman, Francs, II, and Walker Swain. "School Choice, Gentrification, and the Variable Significance of Racial Stratification in Urban Neighborhoods." *Sociology of Education* 90, no. 3 (2017): 213–235.

Perez, Gina. *The Near Northwest Side Story: Migration, Displacement, and Puerto Rican Families.* Berkeley: University of California Press, 2004.

Perlik, Manfred. "Alpine Gentrification: The Mountain Village as a Metropolitan Neighbourhood." *Journal of Alpine Research* 99 (2011). https://journals.openedition.org/rga/1370?gathStatIcon=true&lang=en.

Pettinger, Lynne. "Brand Culture and Branded Workers: Service Work and Aesthetic Labour in Fashion Retail." *Consumption Markets & Culture* 7, no. 2 (2004): 165–184.

Pittman, Cassi. "Shopping while Black: Black Consumers' Management of Racial Stigma and Racial Profiling in Retail Settings." *Journal of Consumer Culture* 20, no. 1 (2017): 3–22.

Pomorski, Chris. "Revitalization Greetings from Asbury Park." *Next City*, August 15, 2016. https://nextcity.org/features/view/new-jersey-asbury -park-redevelopment.

Posey-Maddox, L. *When Middle-Class Parents Choose Urban Schools: Class, Race, and the Challenge of Equity in Public Education.* Chicago: University of Chicago Press, 2014.

Price, David. "7 Policies That Could Prevent Gentrification." Shelterforce, May 23, 2014. https://shelterforce.org/2014/05/23/7_policies_that_could _prevent_gentrification/.

Quillian, Lincoln, Devah Pager, Ole Hexel, and Arnfinn H. Midtboen. "Meta-analysis of Field Experiments Shows No Change in Racial Discrimination in Hiring over Time." *Proceedings of the National Academies of Sciences* 114, no. 41 (2017): 10870–10875. https://doi.org/10.1073/pnas .1706255114.

Raia-Hawrylak, Alicia. "Youth Experiences of Space in a Gentrifying Community: A Case Study of Asbury Park." In *Soul of Society: A Focus on the Lives of Children & Youth*, edited by Mary Nicole Warehime, 1–26. Bingley, U.K.: Emerald Group, 2014.

Randolph, Antonia. *The Wrong Kind of Different: Challenging the Meaning of Diversity in American Classrooms*. New York: Teachers College Press, 2013.

Real Deal. "Asbury Park Likely Buying Beach Property to Stop iStar Development." March 12, 2009. https://therealdeal.com/2019/03/12/asbury -park-looks-at-buying-beach-property-to-stop-istar-development/.

Rizzo, Cailey. "Why Asbury Park Is the Coolest Place on the Jersey Shore." *Travel+Leisure*, July 24, 2018. https://www.travelandleisure.com/trip -ideas/beach-vacations/what-to-do-asbury-park.

RLS Media. "Life Threatening Injuries Reported for Victim of Sewall Avenue Shooting in Asbury Park." July 24, 2019. https://www.rlsmedia.com/ article/life-threatening-injuries-reported-victim-sewall-avenue-shooting -asbury-park.

Roda, Allison. *Inequality in Gifted and Talented Programs: Parental Choices about Status, School Opportunity, and Second-Generation Segregation*. New York: Palgrave Macmillan, 2015.

Rohrer, Finlo. "Why Don't Black Americans Swim?" BBC News, September 3, 2010. https://www.bbc.com/news/world-us-canada-11172054.

Sassen, Saskia. *The Global City: New York, London, Tokyo*. Princeton, N.J.: Princeton University Press, 2001.

Schlichtman, John Joe, Jason Patch, and Marc Lamont Hill. *Gentrifier*. Toronto: University of Toronto Press, 2017.

Schlossbach, Marylin. *Feed This Community: My Life in Food and Community with a Dash of Fun*. Self-published manuscript, 2019. https://www .marilynschlossbach.com/cookbook/feed-this-community-cookbook -soft-cover.

Schuetz, Jenny, Jed Kolko, and Rachel Meltzer. "Are Poor Neighborhoods 'Retail Deserts'?" *Regional Science and Urban Economics* 42, nos. 1–2 (2012): 269–285. https://doi.org/10.1016/j.regsciurbeco.2011.09.005.

Schulz, Dana. "Asbury Park's Second Act: How Developer iStar Is Transforming This Jersey Shore Town." 6SQFT, July 26, 2019. https://www .6sqft.com/asbury-parks-second-act-how-developer-istar-is-transforming -this-jersey-shore-town/.

Scott, Eugene. "Trump's Claim That Black Americans Are Hurt Most by Illegal Immigration Gets Pushback." *Washington Post*, January 9, 2019.

https://www.washingtonpost.com/politics/2019/01/09/trumps-claim
-that-black-americans-are-hurt-most-by-illegal-immigration-gets
-pushback/.

Sherman, Rachel. *Class Acts: Service and Inequality in Luxury Hotels*. Berkeley: University of California Press, 2006.

Simon, Bryant. *Boardwalk of Dreams: Atlantic City and the Fate of Urban America*. New York: Oxford University Press, 2006.

Small, Mario Luis. *Villa Victoria: The Transformation of Social Capital in a Boston Barrio*. Chicago: University of Chicago Press, 2004.

Smith, Michael. "Abercrombie & Fitch under Fire Again for Cool Kids Comment." *Guardian Express*, May 10, 2013. http://guardianlv.com.

Smith, Neil. *The New Urban Frontier: Gentrification and the Revanchist City*. London: Routledge, 1996.

State of New Jersey Department of Education. *New Jersey School Performance Reports 2015–2016 & 2017–2018*. Accessed September 2017 and August 1, 2019. https://rc.doe.state.nj.us/report.aspx?County=25&District=0100& School=010&SchoolYear=2015-2016&SY=1516.

Stillman, Jennifer Burns. *Gentrification and Schools: The Process of Integration When Whites Reverse Flight*. New York: Palgrave Macmillan, 2012.

Strunsky, Steve. "Asbury Park Says Aggressive Panhandling Is 'Embarrassing,' So the City Banned It." NJ.com, October 29, 2018. https://www.nj .com/monmouth/2018/10/asbury_park_bans_aggressive_panhandling .html.

Strupp, Joe. "Asbury Park Schools per Pupil Spending Tops Jersey Shore List Again, Up $5k Each." *Asbury Park Press*, August 9, 2019. https://www .app.com/story/news/education/in-our-schools/2019/08/09/asbury-park -schools-per-pupil-spending-tops-jersey-shore-list-again/1954710001/.

Sullivan, Daniel Monroe, and Samuel Shaw. "Retail Gentrification and Race: The Case of Alberta Street in Portland, Oregon." *Urban Affairs Review* 47, no. 3 (2011): 413–432.

Sundstrom, Mark. "Fatal Police Officer-Involved Shooting in Asbury Park, NJ Reports." WPIX, July 24, 2019. https://pix11.com/2019/07/24/fatal -police-officer-involved-shooting-in-asbury-park-reports/.

Terry, N. "Asbury's Political Power Struggle." *Asbury Park Press*, October 14, 2014. https://www.app.com/story/news/local/eatontown-asbury-park/ asbury-park/2014/10/14/asbury-parks-power-struggle/17276145/.

Thomas, J. "The Gay Bar: Why the Gay Rights Movement Was Born in One." Slate, June 28, 2011. http://www.slate.com/articles/life/the_gay _bar/2011/06/the_gay_bar_4.html?via=rubric_recirc_recent.

Thompson, D. "How Manhattan Became a Rich Ghost Town." *Atlantic*, October 15, 2018. https://www.theatlantic.com/ideas/archive/2018/10/new -york-retail-vacancy/572911/.

Tomaskovic-Devey, Donald. *Gender and Racial Inequality at Work*. Ithaca, N.Y.: ILR Press, 1993.

triCityNews. "Asbury Park's Progressive Approach to Tackle a Major Issue." March 21, 2019, 24, 59.

USA Swimming Foundation. "USA Swimming Foundation Announces 5–10% Increase in Swimming Ability among U.S. Children." May 25, 2017. https://www.usaswimmingfoundation.org/utility/landing-pages/ news/2017/05/25/usa-swimming-foundation-announces-5-10-percent -increase-in-swimming-ability-among-u.s.-children.

U.S. Census Bureau. *Census 2000 Summary File 1, Table DP-1*. Generated by Shawn McMahon using American FactFinder. Accessed July 17, 2019. http://factfinder.census.gov.

———. *Census 2000 Summary File 3, Table DP-4*. Generated by Shawn McMahon using American FactFinder. Accessed July 17, 2019. http:// factfinder.census.gov.

———. *Census 2000 Summary File 3, Table P087*. Generated by Shawn McMahon using American FactFinder. Accessed July 16, 2019. http:// factfinder.census.gov.

———. *2006–2010 American Community Survey 5-Year Estimates, Table B17010*. Generated by Shawn McMahon using American FactFinder. Accessed July 16, 2019. http://factfinder.census.gov.

———. *2006–2010 American Community Survey 5-Year Estimates, Table B25013*. Generated by Shawn McMahon using American FactFinder. Accessed August 28, 2019. http://factfinder.census.gov.

———. *2006–2010 American Community Survey 5-Year Estimates, Table C15002*. Generated by Shawn McMahon using American FactFinder. Accessed July 2, 2019. http://factfinder.census.gov.

———. *2006–2010 American Community Survey 5-Year Estimates, Table S1501*. Generated by Shawn McMahon using American FactFinder. Accessed July 2, 2019. http://factfinder.census.gov.

———. *2006–2010 American Community Survey 5-Year Estimates, Table S1701.* Generated by Shawn McMahon using American FactFinder. Accessed July 16, 2019. http://factfinder.census.gov.

———. *2008–2012 American Community Survey 5-Year Estimates, Table CP03.* Generated by Shawn McMahon using American FactFinder. Accessed July 27, 2019. http://factfinder.census.gov.

———. *2013–2017 American Community Survey 5-Year Estimates, Table B02001.* Generated by Shawn McMahon using American FactFinder. Accessed July 16, 2019. http://factfinder.census.gov.

———. *2013–2017 American Community Survey 5-Year Estimates, Table B05002.* Generated by Shawn McMahon using American FactFinder. Accessed September 5, 2019. http://factfinder.census.gov.

———. *2013–2017 American Community Survey 5-Year Estimates, Table B17010.* Generated by Shawn McMahon using American FactFinder. Accessed July 16, 2019. http://factfinder.census.gov.

———. *2013–2017 American Community Survey 5-Year Estimates, Table B20017.* Generated by Shawn McMahon using American FactFinder. Accessed August 28, 2019. http://factfinder.census.gov.

———. *2013–2017 American Community Survey 5-Year Estimates, Table B25003.* Generated by Shawn McMahon using American FactFinder. Accessed August 28, 2019. http://factfinder.census.gov.

———. *2013–2017 American Community Survey 5-Year Estimates, Table B25013.* Generated by Shawn McMahon using American FactFinder. Accessed August 28, 2019. http://factfinder.census.gov.

———. *2013–2017 American Community Survey 5-Year Estimates, Table C15002.* Generated by Shawn McMahon using American FactFinder. Accessed July 2, 2019. http://factfinder.census.gov.

———. *2013–2017 American Community Survey 5-Year Estimates, Table CP03.* Generated by Shawn McMahon using American FactFinder. Accessed July 27, 2019. http://factfinder.census.gov.

———. *2013–2017 American Community Survey 5-Year Estimates, Table DP04.* Generated by Shawn McMahon using American FactFinder. Accessed July 17, 2019. http://factfinder.census.gov.

———. *2013–2017 American Community Survey 5-Year Estimates, Table DP05.* Generated by Shawn McMahon using American FactFinder. Accessed July 17, 2019. http://factfinder.census.gov.

———. *2013–2017 American Community Survey 5-Year Estimates, Table S0101.* Generated by Shawn McMahon using American FactFinder. Accessed June 20, 2019. http://factfinder.census.gov.

———. *2013–2017 American Community Survey 5-Year Estimates, Table S1501.* Generated by Shawn McMahon using American FactFinder. Accessed July 2, 2019. http://factfinder.census.gov.

———. *2013–2017 American Community Survey 5-Year Estimates, Table S1601.* Generated by Shawn McMahon using American FactFinder. Accessed September 5, 2019. http://factfinder.census.gov.

———. *2013–2017 American Community Survey 5-Year Estimates, Table S1701.* Generated by Shawn McMahon using American FactFinder. Accessed July 16, 2019. http://factfinder.census.gov.

———. *2013–2017 American Community Survey 5-Year Estimates, Table S1901.* Generated by Shawn McMahon using American FactFinder. Accessed August 28, 2019. https://factfinder.census.gov.

U.S. Consumer Financial Protection Bureau. *Home Mortgage Disclosure Act Database.* Accessed July 18, 2019. https://www.consumerfinance.gov/data-research/hmda/.

U.S. Equal Employment Opportunity Commission. "Abercrombie & Fitch Sued for Religious Discrimination." Press release, September 9, 2010. https://www.eeoc.gov/eeoc/newsroom/release/9-1-10.cfm.

Venkatesh, Sudhir. *American Project: The Rise and Fall of a Modern Ghetto.* Cambridge, Mass.: Harvard University Press, 2000.

———. *Gang Leader for a Day: A Rogue Sociologist Takes to the Streets.* New York: Penguin, 2008.

Vigdor, Jacob L., Douglas S. Massey, and Alice Rivlin. "Does Gentrification Harm the Poor?" *Brookings-Wharton Papers on Urban Affairs* (2002): 133–182. https://www.jstor.org/stable/25067387.

Wacquant, Loic. *Urban Outcasts: A Comparative Sociology of Advanced Marginality.* Malden, Mass.: Polity Press, 2008.

Waldinger, Rodger, and Michael Lichter. *How the Other Half Works.* Berkeley: University of California Press, 2003.

Warhurst, Chris, and Dennis Nickson. *Aesthetic Labour.* London: Sage, 2016.

Warhurst, Chris, Chris Tilly, and Mary Gatta. "The New Social Construction of Skills." In *Oxford Handbook of Skills and Training*, edited by John

Buchanan, David Finegold, Ken Mayhew, and Chris Warhurst, 72–91. Oxford: Oxford University Press, 2016.

Waters, Laura. "Are We Getting What We Paid for in Asbury Park Schools?" WHYY, December 3, 2014. https://whyy.org/articles/are-we -getting-what-we-paid-for-in-asbury-park-schools/.

Weber, Mark, and Julia Sass Rubin. "New Jersey Charter Schools: A Data-Driven View—2018 Update, Part I (2018)." Rutgers University Libraries, March 2018. https://doi.org/doi:10.7282/T39Z983M.

Weinberg, Abigail. "Kirsten Gillibrand Has White Privilege and Knows How to Use It." *Mother Jones*, July 31, 2019. https://www.motherjones .com/politics/2019/07/kirsten-gillibrand-has-white-privilege-and-knows -how-to-use-it/.

Weston, Kath. "Get Thee to a Big City: Sexual Imaginary and the Great Gay Migration." *GLQ* 2, no. 3 (1995): 253–277.

Willie, Lois. *At Home in the Loop: How Clout and Community Built Chicago's Dearborn Park*. Carbondale: Southern Illinois University Press, 1998.

Wilson, William Julius. *The Truly Disadvantaged: The Inner City, the Under-class, and Public Policy*. Chicago: University of Chicago Press, 1987.

———. *When Work Disappears: The World of the New Urban Poor*. New York: Vintage, 1997.

Zamudio, Margert, and Michael Lichter. "Bad Attitudes and Good Soldiers: Soft Skills as a Code for Tractability in the Hiring of Immigrant Latina/os over Native Blacks in the Hotel Industry." *Social Problems* 55 (2008): 573–589.

Zillow. "Economic Data." Accessed July 18, 2019. https://www.zillow.com/ research/data/.

Zukin, Sharon. "From Ghetto to Global." In *Global Cities, Local Streets*, edited by Xianming Chen, Phillip Kasinitz, and Sharon Zukin, 29–58. New York: Routledge, 2015.

———. *Naked City: The Death and Life of Authentic Urban Places*. New York: Oxford University Press, 2009.

Index

Page numbers followed by *f* and *t* refer to figures and tables, respectively.

About the Authors

MOLLY VOLLMAN MAKRIS is an associate professor and program coordinator of urban studies at CUNY-Guttman Community College. Her work investigates the intersections of gentrification, urban education, and the lives of youth. Her previous book, *Public Housing and School Choice in a Gentrified City: Youth Experiences of Uneven Opportunity* (2015), won the AESA Critics Choice Book Award.

MARY GATTA is an associate professor at CUNY-Guttman Community College. She is a leader in research on gender, workforce development, and policy. Her most recently published books are *Waiting on Retirement: Aging and Economic Insecurity in Low Wage Work* (2018) and *All I Want Is a Job! Unemployed Women Navigating the Public Workforce System* (2014).